Palestine 1917

Robert Henry Wilson

Edited by Helen D Millgate

Costello

British Library Cataloguing in Publication Data
Wilson, Robert Henry
Palestine 1917.
1. Great Britain. *Army. Royal*
Gloucestershire Hussars Yeomanry—History
2. World War, 1914–1918—Personal
narratives, British 3. World War, 1914–1918
—Campaigns—Palestine
I. Title II. Millgate, Helen D.
940.4′15′0924 D568.7

ISBN 0-7104-3034-5

First published 1987

D J Costello (Publishers) Ltd
43 High Street Tunbridge Wells Kent TN1 1XL

Typeset in Century Old Style by
Composing Operations Ltd Southborough Kent.
Printed and bound in Great Britain by
Billings and Sons Ltd Worcester.

CONTENTS

Foreword by the Marquess of Anglesey   5
Introduction   15

1. Army experiences in England.   17
2. General Introduction to the Middle Eastern campaign
    and to the Royal Gloucestershire Hussars Yeomanry
    in particular.
    En route to Egypt – settling in with the Regiment.   35
3. "Baptism of Fire" at Romani, August 1916.   47
4. Movements in Egypt: action at Rafa – and wounded.   55
5. In hospital Port Said and convalescent at Alexandria.
    Preliminaries and first two battles for Gaza, Spring
    1917.   65
6. Summer 1917 – stalemate – the lighter side of
    desert warfare – General Allenby takes over – on
    course in Cairo and leave in Alexandria.   79
7. Success at Gaza – Cavalry charge at Huj – "Jerusalem
    by Christmas."   89
8. 1918 – significant meeting in Cairo – Spring and
    summer in the Jordan Valley – abortive expedition
    across the Jordan.   103
9. The "Big Push" – the jaws close at Damascus.   121
10. Malaria at Baalbek – Macabre adventures in Beirut
    – end of active service.   145
11. Journey home 1919 – "Hero's welcome?"   161

Postscript.   175

Robert Henry Wilson was born in Shrivenham on 19th January 1894 the fourth son of a well-known farmer dealer. With his younger sister he attended the local dame school and then went to Burford Grammar as a boarder. In 1904 the family moved to Prebendal Farm at Bishopstone on historic Wiltshire downland, where his father leased a sizeable acreage from the Church Commissioners. After leaving school Robert joined his father and three older brothers to work the farm and seems to have enjoyed a full sporting and social life before leaving home, on his twenty-first birthday, to join the Berkshire Yeomanry.

FOREWORD

by The Marquess of Anglesey, D.Litt, FSA, FRHistS, FRSL

Author of *A History of the British Cavalry.*

The three best known British generals of the First World War were all cavalrymen: French, Haig and Allenby. Of these only the last enjoyed any real scope for anything approaching traditional cavalry fighting. Allenby's campaigns against the Turks in the Near East during 1917 and 1918 were the last in the history of the world in which the mobility conferred by men on horseback was successfully employed on a large scale. Never before in the annals of the British army had so numerous a mounted force been employed. The Desert Mounted Corps consisted at times of the equivalent of four divisions, comprising as many as a dozen brigades. There were nearly fifty mounted regiments of one sort or another employed in the course of the campaigns. It took some time for the commanders to master the art of controlling these formations, but they had the inestimable advantage of considerable periods of inaction in which to gain experience as well as possessing staffs which could work together over long periods.

The circumstances which made this unlikely final flowering of the mounted arm possible are worth careful study. The Turks possessed little cavalry worthy of the name. More important, the quality and morale of the Turkish troops rarely compared with that of the Germans and Austrians in the European theatre. Nevertheless the Turkish infantryman was a stubborn and extremely hardy fighter under certain conditions and Allenby never made the mistake of underestimating his enemies, especially as they were commanded in succession by two first-class German generals and included a number of German and Austrian units.

As for weapons, the Turks were well supplied with modern machine guns and they knew how to serve them efficiently. Towards the end of the campaigns their strength in artillery, served mostly, as were also the machine gun units, by Germans and Austrians, was a good deal less than that of the British, but the disparity in guns was nothing like the disparity in mobile forces.

★   ★   ★

Although most of the Sinai Desert consists of flat sand and dunes and though there are considerable open plains in much of Palestine, it would be untrue to suggest that the ground was ideal for cavalry operations. Deep wadis, soft sand and, particularly in the Jerusalem area, numerous steep-sided hills were the chief obstacles to speedy movement by large bodies of horsemen.

★   ★   ★

It is interesting to note that not a single regiment of regular cavalry from home took part in the campaigns. Beside the yeomanry regiments, there were large numbers of Australian and New Zealander light horsemen as well as a few native Indian cavalry regiments. Virtually all the regular cavalry from Britain were fighting as infantry in the trenches of the Western Front or waiting behind the lines for the long expected break-through. Whether the regulars would have done as well as their yeomanry and colonial brothers it is impossible to say. From my studies of their comparative performances in the Boer War, I suspect that neither Allenby nor his predecessor, Sir Archibald Murray, would have happily exchanged, for any number of regulars, the splendid units which served under them. These "irregulars," after all, started from scratch. They, like the Australasians, were considerably less hidebound than the regulars and had had fewer pre-conceived ideas drummed into them. They had far less to un-learn and they were wonderfully quick to absorb the new lessons which the circumstances of modern war forced upon them.

Most of the yeomanry regiments, including Bob Wilson's, the Royal Gloucester Hussars, had fought dismounted at Gallipoli before returning to Egypt at the end of that hapless adventure, (their first-hand knowledge of dismounted action was therefore very wide). But this was before Wilson had joined his regiment from home and by the time he arrived in the theatre his comrades had already been in mounted action. As he says, he found them "in rather a state of depression", for the engagement at Qatia on 23 April 1916 had been an almost unmitigated disaster. Nearly all the mistakes that cavalry could make were made by the three yeomanry regiments involved on that occasion. Qatia was a most salutory lesson; one which was quickly learned.

★   ★   ★

One reason for the success of the mounted troops was the long periods of stalemate, especially during the heat of the summer, when very little fighting took place. This allowed for intensive, prolonged spells of training, not only of individuals, squadrons and regiments, but also of the larger formations. Training of the latter sort had always proved impracticable at home in peacetime, due chiefly to lack of adequate training grounds. It was equally impracticable behind the lines in France, for the vast numbers of casualties on the Western Front and the consequent high turnover of manpower meant that no sooner had one set of men been trained than another had to be speedily and cursorily trained to replace them.

By the time Allenby's classic final advance took place in September 1918 the yeomanry and the Australasians were probably better trained in modern mounted action than any cavalry in history. From the battle of Romani, under Murray, in which Wilson received his baptism of fire, through such long range raids as Chetwode's at Rafa, (where Wilson was galloper to his brigadier) and the brilliant third battle of Gaza, to the famous, if costly, charge at Huj on 8 November 1917, and in numerous minor actions, the mounted troops learned their craft the hard way. What they learned in and out of action they put to glorious effect at Megiddo, *en route* to Damascus and in the final race to Aleppo.

There were some astonishingly long marches made in the course of the campaigns. In one reconnaissance sixty miles were covered in thirty-two hours during the height of the hot weather. Numerous cases of heat exhaustion occurred as a result, nevertheless the men led their horses for much of the way. This was a shining and typical example of good horse-mastership, the art of which had not hitherto been a strong point in cavalry training, but without which the mounted troops' prodigious successes could not have been achieved.

★ ★ ★

The question of remounts was one of transcendant import-ance. In fact most of the horses stood the appalling strains to which they were subjected remarkably well. Except for battle casualties very few, by the standards of earlier wars, had to be evacuated. Extremely careful selection was the secret, for a poor type of horse seldom lasted long. Physical toughness was the prime requirement, especially where soft sand had to be negotiated: it was not uncommon for animals to sink up to their hocks in the sand.

★ ★ ★

Another factor which was new in cavalry operations and which was vital to the success of twentieth-century mounted action was the use of efficient supporting fire-power. All the cavalry formations were equipped with machine gun sections and later on special machine gun squadrons were formed.

When it came to a charge these were generally indispensable for covering fire, but they were even more so when dismounted action had to be resorted to, which happened very often. There were immense problems in getting horse artillery batteries (all of which were Territorial) to keep up with the fast moving squadrons, particularly in heavy going and in the hill country of inland Palestine. When mounted troops charged infantry who were supported by artillery and machine guns, unless they were equally well supported, the charge usually failed, with terrible casualties resulting. Yet, amazingly, there were occasions when the elements of surprise and speed alone so demoralized the enemy that his firing became sufficiently erratic as to have little effect. Indeed, the charges at Beersheba and El Mughar, amongst others, are admirable demonstrations of the saying: "speed is armour".

★   ★   ★

Wilson often touches upon the daunting conditions which were the ever present background to the campaigns in which he took part. The chief restraint upon speedy operations was the chronic shortage of water. The allowance for each man was seldom more than a gallon a day for all purposes and often less. There were occasions, particularly during the frequent dust storms, when the temperature soared above 120°F and parched throats and cracked lips found little relief from occasional sips of the precious fluid. Until the fertile parts of Palestine and Syria were reached, practically all drinking water had to come by means of massive pipelines from the Sweet Water Canal in Egypt, hundreds of miles in the rear. The construction of these and of the railway extensions which ran parallel to them was one of the major feats of organization during the war.

The difficulties of supplying fast-moving mounted masses, sometimes as numerous as 12,000 or more, where few proper roads existed, was another major constraint upon swift movement over long distances. Except for a few limbers, ambulance carts and cable wagons, supply vehicles, both mechanized and horse-drawn, were, more often than not, unable to operate. Consequently thousands of camels and donkeys had to be almost entirely depended upon.

★   ★   ★

Bombing and machine gun attacks from the air were a new unpleasantness. They were especially horrifying for the horses. It took a considerable time before the British achieved superiority in the air. So long as the Turks were supported by modern German machines, there were immense problems connected with hiding concentrations – particularly horses – from aerial reconnaissance. These were increased by the sand clouds which were invariably raised by troop movements in the desert.

Malaria, typhoid, "sand colic" and "gippy tummy" were ever present menaces. These at times reduced most alarmingly the numbers of men available for duty.

★   ★   ★

Other exigencies of desert warfare not, of course, encountered in the static warfare of France, were the inadequacy of detailed maps. Even with the good maps which aerial photography eventually produced, compass reading by day and direction-finding by the stars at night were often essential where there were so few landmarks. For reasons of surprise and to avoid the heat of the day, the incidence of night marching was necessarily very high. Without extensive knowledge of the night sky it would have been impossible for a unit which marched twenty-nine miles, as once happened, in a thick fog over unknown dune country, to succeed in surrounding and capturing an unsuspecting garrison by first light.

★　★　★

The officers and men of the yeomanry who served in Sinai, Palestine and Syria were of a very different type from their predecessors. The constitution of their regiments and their training too, was quite unlike those which existed before the war. Raised originally in 1794 as part of the volunteer forces for helping to repel invasion and for maintaining order in Britain, the yeomanry was treated by Government with indifference during most of the nineteenth century. It was almost entirely due to private and voluntary effort – and money – that the regiments were kept in being at all.

The very idea of a professional body of soldiers was foreign to corps whose chief object after the Napoleonic Wars had always been the suppression of riots and tumults within the counties from which they were raised. Until 1855 the yeomanry was still administered by the Home Department. In that year the War Office took it over, but this did not make much difference to Government attitude.

The yeomanry for the most part consisted of "the Yeoman of England, with noblemen and gentlemen as officers", which was to say tenant farmers and their sons, acting under the command of their landlords and their landlords' sons. In industrial districts the officers were often factory owners and their agents, with small manufacturers, innkeepers and tradesmen in the ranks. By 1914, the proportion of the latter had considerably increased. Since the great agricultural depression late in the nineteenth century a much larger percentage of recruits came from the towns – even more than for the regular cavalry. This was an increasing tendency right up to the outbreak of war. During the war, of course, less suitable men found their way into the yeomanry, though valiant efforts were made to recruit, where possible, good men from the relevant counties.

Initially and for a long time after its foundation, the basic requirement for the yeomanry was that both officers and men should be able to provide a suitable horse and saddlery, either by ownership or on hire, whilst Government provided arms and ammunition. Everything else had to be found by the yeoman himself or by his commanding officer. Until the South African War, for which the Imperial Yeomanry was founded in 1899, yeomanry regiments never went overseas.

★ ★ ★

Though there were far-reaching reforms affecting the economy and constitution of the yeomanry in the 1870s under Cardwell, it was not until Haldane became Secretary of State for War in 1905 that serious steps were taken to transform it into a force capable of fighting alongside the regular army. As late as 1907 official military opinion was unanimous in holding that the yeomanry was quite unfit to take the field against European troops. Four years earlier a distinguished yeomanry officer said that "the only way we shall get the Yeomanry to be of any use is to look upon each regiment as a depot for general service." In effect this is what many of them had become by August 1914. Haldane's great scheme envisaged an additional six regiments as part of the British Expeditionary Force. These units were chiefly designed to act as divisional cavalry for the infantry divisions. The rest, then numbering some 27,000 of all ranks, formed in part a nucleus from which the cavalry of the second line might be formed in time of war, and in part an essential element of the home defence forces.

There was much to be done to bring the regiments out of the excessive amateurism which had hitherto characterized them. Under two far-seeing and energetic Directors of the Territorial Force, Generals McKinnon and Cowans, giant steps were taken to professionalize the yeomanry. By the time regiments arrived in the Middle East, there was not a great deal to distinguish them, (so far as organization, pay, arms and equipment were concerned), from other mounted units of the army. They managed to keep, though, a semblance of terri- torial *esprit de corps* which largely vanished from the regular army, and this served them well in Egypt, Sinai, Palestine and Syria.

★ ★ ★

There are surprisingly few authoritative and readable personal accounts from officers and men who fought there. Bob Wilson's reminiscences are therefore most welcome. They are especially interesting because of the light they shed upon the day to day experiences of all ranks. It is his record of these which induce in the reader a feeling of knowing what it was really like to be there. The alternate bouts of elation and dejection, of tedium and anxiety are exceedingly well depicted. It so happens, too, that Wilson was a particularly likeable specimen of the old yeoman class and a remarkable person in his own right.

Helen Millgate has edited his letters and his commentaries with consummate skill. Her connecting narrative is exactly what is required and it tells us just what we need to know about the background. Without question this book is an important addition to the literature of the most important "sideshow" of the First World War.

Acknowledgements

My thanks to my friend Alice Zeitlyn, the daughter of Josephine Davies, for introducing me to Robert Henry Wilson, to Mrs Cherry Hopkins of the Cambridge Reference Library for steering me in the right direction and to Sibyl Crowe and Geoffrey Fisher who kindly looked over the finished manuscript.

For Paddie . . .

Introduction

I was a keen student of military matters before I was six years old and took the greatest interest in anything to do with the South African war. I wore in my buttonholes picture badges of Lord Roberts, General French, Buller and Baden Powell and was determined to get out there as soon as possible. My desire to have my own Regiment had prompted me to design a regimental uniform, entirely unserviceable but full of glamour. I had a box of toy soldiers in two ranks; the front kneeling, the rear standing, rifles at the ready. The front rank I called "Squatters" and the rear "Standers".

One day I went with my father to buy some sheep from a farmer and when his wife offered me a stool to sit down on I said: "No thank you, I'm a Stander not a Squatter." Then she asked: "What are you going to be when you grow up?" Drawing myself to my full two feet and six inches I scornfully replied: "Grow up? I'll be under the ground in South Africa long before I have a chance to grow up." I remember the bells ringing for the relief of Ladysmith, the excitement and joy when Mafeking was liberated, and my father rushing upstairs to change his clothes so that he could catch a train from Swindon to join the celebrations in London.

Added to the frustration of not being able to go to South Africa, I suffered two major disappointments. We had been promised that, when the war was over, we should have the privilege of seeing President Kruger hauled around all the villages in a cage, as if he were some sort of menagerie specimen. I felt badly let down by his non-appearance. The other was more of a shock than a disappointment. The gallant Bugler Dunn had been awarded the Victoria Cross and his name was on everyone's lips. My father, in his frequent bursts of patriotism, was in the habit of singing some song about some boy trumpeter who I equated with Dunn the Bugler Boy. I was certain that whatever they could do I could do better assuming that they were men of my own age: about six or seven. Then one day the newspaper included a war magazine called *The Black and White Budget* which contained pictures of those who had lost their lives or distinguished themselves in some way. My mother, who had been studying the papers, suddenly said "There's Bugler Dunn the V C." I rushed to have a look but could not see any seven year old "boy" only a little man with a walrus moustache and a pill box hat on a completely bald pate. I was stunned.

Perhaps this disillusionment with things military explains the fact that when I did eventually join the army I became the most useless, undisciplined and unorthodox member of His Majesty's forces; as the RSM said: "You are the worst bloody trooper I have met in 35 years soldiering. "

Chapter 1

On January 19th 1915, my 21st birthday, feeling that at last I was free – and knowing only too well that I should have gone months before – I slipped away to join the Berkshire Yeomanry. Although this was the most crucial day of my life it was also one of the most amusing. There was one other recruit, a man named Cook, a gamekeeper and some years older than me. After having caps without badges banged on our heads and being given uniforms with unpolished buttons, the traditional [King's] shilling and a railway warrant, we were told to march to the station to join the regiment. The recruiting sergeant had told us that we were now soldiers – a gross overstatement – and that we should now look out for officers and be sure to salute them. So the two new soldiers marched up the main street of Reading with our civilian clothes in a newspaper parcel and, to satisfy our conceit, halted for a few seconds to see our reflections in a shop window. We were so horrified at what we saw that we felt like running to the station.

Officers were plentiful that morning and, when we met the first one, Cookie remembered what the sergeant had told us but, instead, raised his cap – without removing the huge carved pipe from his mouth. I got him to a doorway and told him that no doubt the officer would overlook the raising of his cap as a substitute for a salute but I thought the pipe was going a bit far. He duly changed over to a cigarette and when the next officer appeared Cookie's hand was halfway to his cap when I said "Your fag, Cookie." He only succeeded in jamming the burning cigarette into his mouth and spitting and spluttering whilst the officer walked past. Dear Cookie, we parted in 1916 when I got my Commission.

We were in the second line of the Berkshire Yeomanry, the first line being at full strength on mobilisation, and were billeted in a huge mansion called 'Bearwood' just outside Reading. My brother Ted had joined us and we were, of course, 'troopers'. As far as merit was concerned we should have so stayed but due to the fact that our squadron leader was a very close friend, Master of Lady Craven's Harriers and joint Master of the old Berks Hunt – country in which our farms were situated – we gradually reached the rank of lance corporal – unpaid. As a trooper my first pay day netted me five shillings and fourpence and I told the sergeant major that I thought I was at least in the bob-a-day category but he simply said, "One and eightpence stopped for breakages." I hadn't been there long enough to break anything but he showed very commendable foresight as I was, in due course, to break every possible rule that ever appeared in King's Regulations.

This was soldiering in its very lowest form, far removed from the glamour and heroics that I had pictured during the Boer War when I was six years old. Although we were supposed to be a cavalry regiment we had no horses – but we all had to wear spurs. The recruits from the towns fell over these spurs as often as they fell off their horses when they eventually arrived. Boredom was complete; it all seemed such a waste of time after the busy lives we had led at home.

My brother Ted was bright enough to create a separate command of his own. One of the officers, Captain Crundell, a motor enthusiast, got on very well with Ted and let him tinker about with his cars. So Ted bought a motor bike and suggested that Captain Crundell should persuade the colonel that he really ought to have a despatch rider, and that he knew of one who was already equipped with a motor bike. The colonel was rather flattered and agreed at once. Ted was issued with a pair of goggles, and to all intents and purposes reverted to private life. He never appeared on parade again but would occasionally be seen sailing past, with a pretty Irish nurse from the hospital riding pillion.

As time went on we were issued with rifles which were coated with the most filthy looking grease, so repulsive in appearance and smell that I accepted mine with finger and thumb. The quartermaster was foolish enough to say that they had been stored in that condition for 15 years and no harm had come to them. I decided that mine should remain in that condition for another 15 years and, if any harm should come to it, I couldn't care less! I certainly wasn't going to clean the wretched thing; when I was on guard duty I used to borrow one from the cooks. Guard duties were a farce. There were three sentry boxes; one by the main entrance and the other two on minor gateways. The orderly officer was most punctual and always appeared at 10pm; we knew that after that it was safe to leave our posts and withdraw to the guard-room to drink beer and play cards for the rest of the night.

One beautiful spring morning I thought I should like a breath of fresh air and, as everyone else was asleep, I picked up a rifle with bayonet attached, lit my pipe and went for a stroll along the front of the mansion. When it became lighter I realised that I was rather conspicuous, being in full view of all the officers' windows, so I decided to occupy the sentry box at the main gate. I leant the rifle in one corner, sat down and covered myself with my great-coat preparing for a little beauty sleep. I gradually became aware that I was being observed by someone and it turned out to be none other than Colonel J B Karslake, who I believe was MP for Paddington, was over 6ft 6ins tall, always immaculately turned out and never without a huge monocle and an outsize bicycle that he'd had specially built. I staggered to my feet and picked up the rifle. I remembered that one should present arms to the colonel, but he was standing too close to allow me to get outside so I decided to do the best I could from inside. I flung up the rifle with such zeal that the bayonet stuck firmly in the roof and all my tugging failed to remove it. The best thing I could do was to stand stiffly to attention with the wretched rifle dangling about in front of my face. By this time I had become slightly embarrassed and the fact that the colonel remained absolutely silent, though probably fascinated, by the display, added to my embarrassment. Finally: "What's your name?" "Wilson, Sir." "Squadron?" "C Squadron, Sir." "You will hear more of this." No doubt he told Major Nickisson, my hunting squadron leader, to have me shot at dawn – but I heard no more about it.

The aim of everyone was to escape the day by day boredom so, when the entire regiment was on the parade ground one afternoon and the squadron sergeant major came up to me and said: "You speak French, don't you?" I immediately sensed something to my advantage and said "Yes, sir." Just as the Colonel gave the order "Section: right, quick march" the sergeant major shouted: "Trooper Wilson, fall out." I dropped to the rear and, when the regiment had disappeared from sight, he came across to tell me to get ready to go into Reading as he wanted to take two Belgian refugee girls out to tea. This was a great improvement on a route march on a cold January afternoon. He explained on the way that I was required simply because his French was not "very hot." I had grave doubts about my own.

When we arrived at the house, I was saddened to see about twenty Belgian ladies of all ages in the one room. The only furniture was a table which had on it a large pot of jam, two loaves of bread, one knife and one spoon. It was not surprising that the girls wanted to be taken out for tea. My worst fears were realised when we found it quite impossible to exchange a single word as they spoke Flemish. Fortunately the sergeant major knew the names of the two lucky girls, Marie and Marcelle, so we were able to nudge them away from the rest of the party. I don't think it was mere coincidence that they happened to be the youngest and prettiest of the lot: the old man had obviously carried out some reconnaissance. He was the most gentle NCO I had ever met; a huge man who had represented Britain in the Olympic Games heavyweight boxing. He reached the final and would probably have won but for the fact that he had already fought another tough bout the same day.

The tea party was a great success despite the complete absence of any conversation. The advantage accruing to me was the fact that two or three days a week, and every Saturday, I would get the order to 'Fall out and prepare for tea.' This routine continued for some months until we were moved to a camp under canvas.

As the weather improved we moved to Churn Camp where we began to assume a more soldierly outlook. We were under canvas, the horses had arrived and by the end of the summer we were ready to take our place at the front; fit, tough and well-officered. We then experienced a set back, instead of going overseas, as we had hoped, we were moved up to King's Lynn and dotted about in good billets with its most hospitable population. The flesh-pots were again available, pictures, dances, theatres and, although we were supposed to be in our billets by 10pm, there were no means of ensuring that we were; we soon became soft, disgruntled and discipline just went to the winds. In November 1915 when we were anticipating a snug comfortable winter in our billets, we received a shock. It was decided that the entire regiment would be accommodated in – of all places – the disused workhouse, and the entire regiment decided that it would not. Fatigue parties were sent there daily to get the place tidied up and ready to receive us. This work was always done with "tongue in cheek" as we had no intention of moving in but we underestimated the power and cunning of the regular Regimental Sergeant Major Tommy Lester. He was typical of his rank with an unlimited capacity for beer but always on top of his job and he was to give us a neat and efficient demonstration of how to break up a mutiny.

The order eventually came that we should parade in the Town Gardens situated close to the workhouse at 2 o'clock complete with kit and equipment. That order, of course, had to be obeyed but the fact that it was fixed for a Saturday afternoon indicated at once that our determination not to move had reached the ears of authority, and we scented cowardice as nearly all the officers were on leave at week-ends. This suspicion was confirmed when we found ourselves in the charge of the orderly sergeant. No sign of an officer or the regimental sergeant major – it all seemed so easy. It was fair enough when the orderly sergeant said "Shun"; "Pick up your kit bags" was fair enough too and we obliged; then "Right turn, quick march" and no one moved. He repeated the order three or four times but still no one moved and we felt that we had won the day.

It was at this point that the RSM emerged from an adjacent garden with about ten military policemen. The police lined up behind us, while he took up a position about 20 yards in front. He glared at us with a look of scorn and disgust and applied every adjective in his vocabulary to insult – what he called – the worst bloody example of Fred Karno's Army he'd ever seen. We were beginning to feel a bit shaken and I was wondering what would happen when he ceased abusing us and gave the order to "Quick march"; but he was too wise an old fox to take that risk. He walked up to a little man, "Tubby" Brown, who was about three files from me, placed his nose within about two inches of Tubby's and then, with a roar like a lion, yelled: "Brown, pick up your kit and proceed to the workhouse." Poor Tubby yielded and when he had gone out of sight, the RSM dealt with one or two more in the same way, and eventually the whole mob of us were dribbling away like a host of refugees. I don't know what would have happened if he had picked on me instead of Tubby Brown and, although I was one of the ring leaders of the revolt and his particular "problem child", I don't think I should have had the courage to defy him. However, neither my brother Ted nor I ever spent a night in the new quarters. We came to an arrangement with our landlady to stay on and soon the house was full of cronies who found the damp, cold, evil-smelling workhouse intolerable.

The regimental sergeant major who had dealt so efficiently with this silly situation retired soon afterwards. We had all been very good friends off parade, and when he accepted our invitation to a farewell party we bought him a great deal of beer and sang "For he's a jolly good fellow" as indeed he was. He was succeeded by another regular soldier with 35 years service and from the start we did no get on well. One incident made matters worse. Four of us wanted to go to the Fatstock Show at Smithfield and, as I knew it would be useless to ask the RSM to get our passes signed, I asked the orderly sergeant to slip them to my friendly squadron leader who I knew would not refuse me.

When the RSM's attention was temporarily distracted the orderly sergeant handed them to Major Nickisson who just glanced at the names, scribbled his signature and sent them back to me. When the RSM discovered I had pulled a fast one he went up to Major Nickisson and said, "Beg pardon, Sir, but have you just signed some passes?" When told he had done so, the RSM said "We already have about twenty men on the sick list, a lot of extra duties and we are reduced to one man to two horses and it is impossible to allow any more 48 hour passes." "Oh," said Major Nickisson, "Get me a blue pencil and fetch the passes back from Wilson." The look of satisfaction on the RSM's face was equalled only by the disappointment on mine as I handed them back. He went, collected a blue pencil and returned to Major Nickisson who, again, scribbled on the passes. If ever a man looked like a whipped dog it was poor old RSM Trowbridge that afternoon; written in huge letters from one corner to the other was just one, blue-pencilled word "Special".

The wrath of the RSM which I knew was to come occupied my mind on the train back to King's Lynn after the Smithfield show. This journey was also nerve racking for another reason. One of our group, Tylee Norman, had collected a two-gallon jar of home-made sloe gin from his people at the Show and this was obviously a very precious piece of luggage.

The train from Liverpool Street was always over-crowded with soldiers and sailors returning from leave and I was fearful for the jar of sloe gin in such company. I had carried out a reconnaissance before the train set off and found an empty first class compartment in the next carriage. The corridor door was locked to prevent any infiltration from the third class to the first, so the four of us decided that we would have to get out onto the running board as soon as the train started and transfer by that route to the first class compartment.

As usual I was "muggins" and had to go first, with the jar of gin hanging from my shoulder by a strap. The night was pitch black, the train was travelling at sixty or seventy miles an hour and the rush of cold air, smoke and dust that I encountered as soon as I stepped outside nearly unshipped me. I had no control over the jar at all as both hands were fully occupied maintaining a hold, and I could not stop it banging against the windows as I sidled along the running board.

Eventually I reached the end of the carriage and had to negotiate the gap to the next one. Although it was too dark to see anything, I knew that there were bumpers on each carriage which would help me to step from one to the other; with the vacuum hose representing a very chancy safety net. I waited for a few moments to see if I was being followed, straddling between the two carriages, and then progressed until I found the empty compartment. There was still one big problem: the door had to be opened towards me. I was prepared for trouble when the door flew open but the impact was even more violent than I had expected. However, instead of knocking me off the catwalk, it pushed me flat against the train and I was wedged between the door and the window. I could not even spare a hand to jettison the jar which would have been the most sensible thing to do in the circumstances. It seemed that the engine driver was going flat out and must have been having the time of his life. I looked back to see if anyone had tried to follow me but all I could see was a row of heads at the windows I had passed and nearly smashed with the jar.

Some time later the ticket collector came in, touched his hat, and said, "Good evening, Sir." Then he noticed the one stripe and his attitude changed abruptly. "And how in Hell did you get here?" When I told him he was quite incredulous and said it was not possible. However the jar with the tin mug on the top of it seemed to interest him and he stayed for half an hour in which time we became the best of friends! A pity the rest of the party derived more satisfaction from the survival of the sloe gin than of me.

I was soon to encounter trouble from RSM Trowbridge again. Horses were very scarce and we had a number of remounts from Canada. Not only were they old and unbroken but some were literally wild animals; to groom them required a team of three or four men and to shoe them was virtually impossible. Six of us had been detailed to break them in and we were known as the "Rough Riders", but I don't remember if that was an official title or one we had assumed ourselves. One big advantage was that it enabled us to dodge parades.

One brute about 13 years old and of nearly 17 hands had apparently never been touched. We were determined to get some shoes on this particular horse and I had managed to get a rope over his head and armed myself with a shackling peg, half wood and half iron, weighing about 7lbs which I think would have felled him. When I was in control at his head I was to give the others the tip and they would try and get some ropes round his hind legs, so that we could throw him. I took my eyes off him for a fraction of a second, to signal the others, when he turned like a flash and bit my stomach, shook me like a dog would have a rat, and then threw me about ten yards. I was winded and knocked out and, when I was able to look at my stomach, I could see that he had torn off a piece of skin as big as my hand and I was bleeding like a pig. The doctor had to patch me up; and told me that on no account was I to do any duty for a week.

All men on sick list had to be in their billet by 5pm. It so happened that I had arranged to take one of the sisters from the hospital to the cinema that evening. She was rather late arriving, the cinema was in complete darkness and we were told to take two seats along a certain row. After treading on toes and falling over knees we eventually found the seats and settled down to enjoy the picture. I had just finished telling the sister about my mishap and what the "so and so" sergeant major would do if he knew I was at the pictures when the light went up – she was sitting between me and RSM Trowbridge! He did not speak but, as he and his lady friend got up to leave, he made a special effort to tread on my toes and hit my boney knees.

He sent for me the next morning and I met him with a smile, prepared for anything. "A man who can be in the cinema at 11 o'clock at night is fit to parade in the morning. Saddle up and fall in." There was to be a parade of the whole division and the regiment was very much below strength. I should have been in hospital and was quite incapable of getting on a horse. To convince him I undid my shirt and showed the blood-stained bandages and terrible bruises. All he said was "Good God" then, "Can you ride a motor bike?" My brother Ted's despatch riding squad had by now increased to six but there were only four men available – an added headache for poor Trowbridge. I had never ridden a motor bike in my life – except pillion – but said I would try. I hadn't the slightest idea how to deal with the bike and, after several false starts, Ted decided to abandon me and go ahead with the others. I didn't want to let Trowbridge down so I kept trying and managed to get 100 yards or so before coming to a coughing halt amidst clouds of smoke. All this time I was trying to overtake a least three other cavalry regiments in narrow lanes and was being cursed by everyone. One colonel, who I had overtaken three times, had the nerve to say that I didn't know how to ride a motorcycle and suggested I chuck the damned thing into the ditch! That only served to spur me on and at last I reached the field where the parade was to take place – the bike for some reason, now going really well.

The entire division was assembled and there was tension in the air as the inspecting general and his staff appeared. I had no idea where Ted's gang were supposed to be and, of course, took the wrong line, did a triumphal circular tour of the whole parade and then found the despatch riders within 20 yards of the gate by which I had entered the field. As soon as the general had passed our little party Ted said, "Now, for Heaven's sake, get out of the way as fast as you can." He gave me a few instructions and I felt more confident, so much so that when "Cissie" Bowen – our bank manager's son – said, "Race you back to Lynn." I was only too eager to accept the challenge. I had no idea what speed we were going but Ted, who was terrified to see Bowen and myself vanish out of sight, said we were doing at least 65mph – which in 1915 was pretty good. Bowen was leading by about 100 yards when he did several complete somersaults, like a shot rabbit. I only avoided him by inches and, looking out of the corner of my eye, felt sure he was dead. I must have gone another half mile before I was able to slow down sufficiently to turn round and come back to him. The inner tube of his front wheel had come out and was blown up to the size of forty footballs: a thing I have never seen before or since. The others eventually came along and, as the accident had taken place close to a pub, we carried Bowen and his bike round to the back and were safely out of sight before the column of troops – nearly three miles long – began to ride past. Ted was ungrateful enough to say that he knew what was meant when they called me "Rough Rider". However, I think Trowbridge was somewhat placated by my turning out in the condition I was in and I heard no more about being out of my billet after 5pm.

It was the usual practice at this time when one had had enough of this useless type of soldiering, to apply for a Commission. Such a step was even more desirable in my case as I was continually in some sort of trouble. I asked Regimental Sergeant Major Trowbridge to arrange for me to see the commanding officer to ask his permission for me to make an application. He immediately said "I should not go to the trouble if I were you; I have just decided to offer you a very special job in the Regiment." I was puzzled but not altogether fooled as I was quite sure that he had some sinister motive. He said I was to see him in his office after parade, and when I arrived the Veterinary Surgeon was there too. Trowbridge said, "This is Lance Corporal Wilson, Sir, and he is placed under your orders." There had been a sudden and serious outbreak of mange among the horses – at least 30, and eventually 60 were affected – it is the most filthy skin disease in the horse world and had, no doubt, originated with the Canadian remounts. I was told that I was being put in charge of these horses, and that I could pick five other men to help me and that the horses would be isolated outside the town. This appeared to be rather an attractive proposition as it meant that we would also be isolated and away from the prying eyes of authority. The five men I asked for were all farmer's sons and were readily made available by their Squadron Leaders as – like me – they were constantly giving trouble.

We set about the job quite conscientiously for the horses' sake but it was a loathsome affair and although we were making some complete cures the numbers were continually rising. We were reaching a stage of exhaustion ourselves as half of our party had to be on duty every night, which meant one night on and one night off. I pointed this out to the Vet and asked him to agree to one man doing duty all night and having the next day off. He did not like the idea and said it would not work but that we could give it a try. He was no fool, and when we arrived at 6 o'clock the next morning, he was already there. My heart sank at the sight of the horse lines, some loose, some tangled and no guard in sight. In short everything was wrong. He quietly said, "The new plan doesn't appear to be very successful, Wilson." I agreed, apologised and then went, with the others, to get the horses some hay. We grabbed a bale each from the stack – and out rolled the guard and a lady! We were naturally disappointed at this let-down and, without any orders from the Vet, I used the authority of my single stripe for the first and last time, and the night guard reverted to its proper function. We succeeded in restoring all the horses to a healthy condition and they were duly returned to the ranks. This was the one and only work of any value that I contributed to the Army while I was in England.

I then made up my mind to apply for a commission, the only formality involved was to sign a form and to be interviewed by a single senior officer. If you did not pick your nose during this interview and could solemnly swear that you had hunted with the Old Berks Hounds and Lady Craven's Harriers you were started off in pursuit of a field marshal's baton. In due course I was ordered to present myself before Colonel, The Lord Long who had just relinquished command of the Wiltshire Yeomanry and who could not have been kinder or more considerate.

Before my commission came through I was graced with a special piece of luck. The MO said I should have six teeth out and gave me a ticket to go and see the Army dentist. I was waiting my turn in the hall when the previous customer appeared at the top of the stairs, holding his head with both hands and looking like a bleeding ghost. He passed me without a glance and ran out of the door. I had made up my mind to follow his example, and was just reaching for my cap, when a voice rang out fom the top of the stairs, "Come on you!" I looked up and saw what was obviously the dentist but who looked like a butcher. He was wearing a white smock that was covered with blood and had a murderous looking weapon in his hand, which suggested that the previous patient had made a bolt for it while his back was turned. His first words when I went into the room were, "I hate this bloody job. I had been in the trenches for three months before they discovered I was a dentist and sent me home. I was far happier there." I was bold enough to tell him that I imagine he had been of more use there as well.

The operation left me somewhat toothless in front and he offered to make me a temporary set "on the side" for a mere fiver. He made such a good job of it that they were better than my official set and I used them all through my active service. When I gave him the fiver I told him that I was sorry our business had ended because I had found the few afternoon appointments a great relief from the boredom I was suffering. "Don't let that worry you," he said, "Just fill in one of these bloody things when you want a half day off," and gave me a whole book of appointment forms!

Only a matter of days later, when I was doing corporal of the guard at the workhouse, I received a message to report to the RSM's office. I found him sitting at his green baize table and he said, "Well Wilson, your commission has come through, and here is your railway warrant to enable you to report to the Royal Gloucestershire Hussars Yeomanry." Then with a fatherly expression he added, "Now that we are parting I should like to say one more thing. Of all the men in the regiment worthy of a commission I think you are outstanding." I was so impressed by this apparent change of heart that I foolishly said, "Thank you very much Sir, that is very pleasing, because I admit that occasionally I have been something of a nuisance to you; but why should you say so?" "Because you are the worst bloody soldier I have encountered in 35 years experience." I appreciated that very pretty piece of typical sergeant major's sarcasm and even said "Thank you very much, Sir, I shall remember that as long as I live."

It is strange that, during this period of lack of discipline and shocking behaviour on my part, I always had the greatest admiration for the men who did behave themselves and for the officers and NCOs who tried to make something of me. But I just could not work up any enthusiasm for this type of soldiering. Yet when, later on, the time came for me to be reponsible for the discipline of my own troop – and for a short time a squadron – I experienced no difficulty as every man was keen and willing and I never had occasion to reprimand anyone. Many of them had left a home and life similar to my own and must have had the same feeling that they were wasting their time. Perhaps the difference in our attitudes to the job in hand can be attributed to the image of hero worship and glory that was always before me as a small child. It was the complete disillusionment that soured me. When eventually I was on active service the old enthusiasm and excitement returned and, except for the sometimes intolerable heat of the desert and sometimes distressing shortage of water, I can truthfully say that I enjoyed parts of the war immensely. Fortunately the memories of the comic incidents have almost ousted the few sad and tragic episodes; and these I shall avoid as far as possible.

After a short spell at the Yeomanry depot in Gloucester I was attached to the 4th/7th Dragoon Guards at Tidworth for further training – and, at last, I woke up. Here were the soldiers of my dreams. Total cavalry soldiers from the colonel down to the last recruit; many of them returned warriors – wounded at Mons or afterwards – doing their damnedest to get themselves fit and back to the regiment. Every tradition and etiquette was strictly observed as if the peace had never been disturbed. Ex-rankers were treated as equals and, although the regular officers always wore mess kit in the evenings, we were told in the nicest possible way that we were on no account to spend our money on such things. A white shirt and black tie to wear in the evenings – if we could manage it – would be quite sufficient. My first night happened to be a guest night and one of the traditions of the regiment was that the most recently joined officer should propose the Royal Toast. I was taken aside by the senior subaltern who very apologetically told me that, although he knew it would be something of an ordeal, he was sure the colonel would wish me to take the responsibility. I had to sit at the opposite end of the table – as long as a cricket pitch – from the colonel and, at a signal from the very helpful senior subaltern, rose and did my stuff. The manner in which the warrant officers and senior NCOs accepted us was, without exception, perfectly correct. Although we were constantly under them for drill and instruction I never heard a word of abuse or sarcasm and they were willing to give us hours of their spare time on any subject we found particularly difficult.

We had some of the finest horses; mine was a roan mare for which an officer – still in France – had given £550 for point-to-point and hunting and which was the best I had ever ridden. For 5/– a day, as insurance, we were allowed – rather encouraged – to hunt with the Tadworth. The mess food was excellent and drink of all sorts available; but the serious way in which we were all getting down to the job, and the example set by the Dragoon Guards, ruled out any heavy drinking. We were able for the first time to live within our pay and also, for the first time, I found myself looking forward to getting on parade instead of resorting to every device and trick to dodge them.

I was in due course posted to the Gloucester Yeomanry who were in Egypt and put in charge of about 20 NCOs and men joining the regiment as reinforcements. We were due to leave

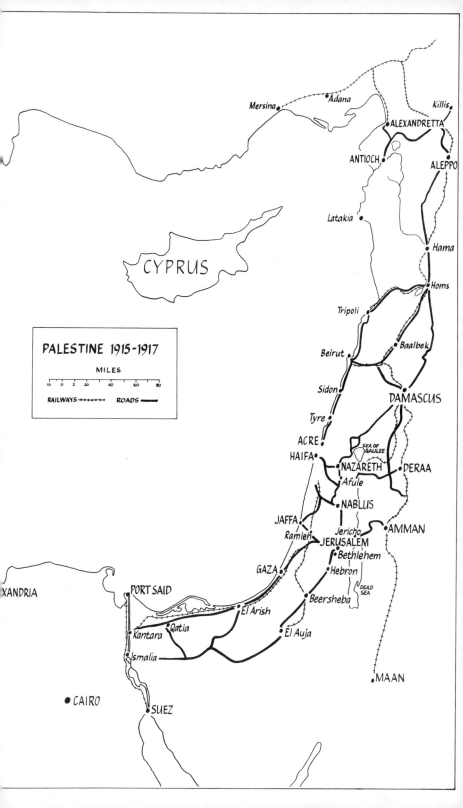

PALESTINE 1915-1917

MILES

10 0 2 20   40   60   80

RAILWAYS ·+·+·+·+·   ROADS ▬▬▬

CYPRUS

Mersina
Adana
Killis
ALEXANDRETTA
ANTIOCH
ALEPPO
Latakia
Hama
Homs
Tripoli
Baalbek
Beirut
Sidon
DAMASCUS
Tyre
ACRE
HAIFA
SEA OF GALILEE
NAZARETH
DERAA
Afule
JAFFA
NABLUS
Ramleh
Jericho
AMMAN
JERUSALEM
GAZA
Bethlehem
Hebron
DEAD SEA
Beersheba
XANDRIA
PORT SAID
El Arish
El Auja
Kantara
Qatia
Ismalia
MAAN
CAIRO
SUEZ

Tidworth Station at 1am. The usual traditions were going to be observed; personal inspection and address by the commanding officer and a full regimental band to lead us to the station. As the men had been paid up to date I was very concerned as to the condition that some of the men might be in by that time. I checked up on them several times during the evening and was, each time, reassured by a dear old corporal – a Boer War veteran named Corporal Wiltshire – that I could rely on him to see that everything was in order. When the time came for the commanding officer's inspection Wiltshire was only kept upright by the aid of three Dragoons. His mess tin was hanging from his neck and he kept tapping it and informing the commanding officer that this was one decoration that he, the commanding officer, had not got! Poor Wiltshire was killed at Rafa.

Chapter 2

The regiment in which Robert Wilson had been granted a commission and to which he was now en route, was the Royal Gloucestershire Hussars Yeomanry, founded in 1830, absorbed into the Territorial Army in 1908, and now fulfilling a cavalry role with the Territorials. In April 1915 the regiment was posted to Egypt as part of the Mediterranean Expeditionary Force then under the command of General Sir Ian Hamilton, General Officer Commanding Egypt.

The situation in the Middle East at the time was highly complex. British influence predominated by virtue of, since 1882, the British occupation of Egypt, although that country was still nominally under the suzerainty of the Ottoman Empire. Britain thus controlled the Suez Canal and retained a strong naval presence in the Mediterranean. However the 19th century "scramble for Africa" had not yet ended and the entire continent was continually subject to the political machinations of the European powers. Apart from the British interest France, Italy and particularly Germany, were constantly manoeuvering for advantage.

Germany had been assidiously courting Turkey for some years, seeking political and commercial favours; the most notable undertaking being the construction of the Hejaz railway. They had also long been involved in a scheme for a Berlin to Bagdad link. The German Military Mission in Turkey was also active in the reorganisation of the Turkish Army and in 1913 Liman von Sanders – who was later to conduct the defence of Gallipoli – was appointed head of the Mission and created field marshal in the Turkish Army.

Upon the outbreak of war in 1914 the Suez Canal became even more vital to Britain to speed the flow of troops and supplies from

India and the Antipodes. On November 5th, when Turkey entered the war on the side of the Central Powers, the situation became somewhat clearer. The vulnerability of Egypt itself, the Sudan, and Aden, commanding the entrance to the Red Sea, became a major cause of concern for the British who were responsible for these territories.

In December 1914 the British government opportunely took advantage of the absence of the pro-Turkish Khedive, Abbas Himli, on a long visit to Turkey, to declare Egypt a British Protectorate. They replaced him with – as Sultan – his uncle, the more amenable Prince Husain Kamil.

There were still threats to be countered from other quarters; for example the revolts by Senussi and the Sultan Dufar, in the winter of 1915 and spring of 1916, in a concerted effort to gain independence for the Sudan. These were successfully overcome as were attempts by Turkish forces to capture Aden.

The greatest threat however occurred when, immediately upon Turkey's entry into the war, the Sultan of Turkey, as titular head of Orthodox Islam, declared a "Jihad", a holy war against the Infidel. Egypt itself being naturally opposed to Turkey and by now filling up with British and Commonwealth troops, was not particularly fertile ground. More crucial would be the response of the vassal sherifs of Arabia. The leader of these, by virtue of his possession of the Holy cities Mecca and Medina, was Emir Hussein Ibn Ali. The onset of war had already stopped the flow of pilgrims to Mecca and the Emir, reliant on food ships from India, was in any event reluctant to become an enemy of Britain. Moreover, according to T E Lawrence, he was an honourable and deeply pious man who could not reconcile the idea of a religious war being used to pursue secular aims. His refusal to concur marked the real beginnings of the Arab Revolt which crystallised in the summer of 1916; a long-held dream to free Arabia from Turkish rule.

Initiated early in 1915, at Russia's request to re-open the Dardenelles to her shipping, was the abortive and costly Gallipoli campaign. Another of these "Imperial Sideshows" was the Mesopotamian expidition undertaken to guard the Anglo-Persian oil fields and to prevent enemy incursions into the Indian Ocean. The capture of Basra was successful but an ill-considered advance up the Tigris led to the infamous siege at Kut. Later in 1915 came the humiliating Macedonian affair when hundreds of thousands of Allied troops occupied Salonika for almost three years, to no real purpose.

Egypt was effectively the base for all these operations (from June 1915 to spring 1916 known as the Levant Base) and it was to this great pool of men and resources that the First Regiment Royal Gloucester Hussars were despatched. After some weeks spent acclimatising and undergoing further training the regiment (less one hundred men) received orders to embark – dismounted – for Mudros, the advance base for Gallipoli on the island of Lesbos. From there they proceeded to Sulva Bay suffering heavy losses in action at Chocolate Hill. Many more were evacuated because of sickness and, when they eventually returned to Alexandria in November, the regiment was considerably under-strength, numerically and physically. The entire regiment was then sent to Mena Camp near Cairo to retrain as a mounted unit and to be re-inforced.

In March 1916 Sir Archibald Murray took command of the newly formed Egyptian Expeditionary Force. He envisaged a defensive role but felt this could best be achieved, not close to the Suez Canal, but at El Arish, a strategic town on the Mediterranean coast with access to good water supplies and some 28 miles from the frontier with Palestine. To effect this advance across the Sinai Peninsular, to move and support an army of sufficient size and strength, necessitated the construction of a single-track railway, tracks for motorised vehicles and, above all, a secure water supply. This vast undertaking was already under way when the

Royal Gloucester Hussars were sent from Kantara on the Canal to Romani – a position about 20 miles to the east – in advance of the rail link and to protect its construction.

On April 23rd, A Squadron, whilst temporarily guarding camp at Qatia five miles away, was attacked by a superior Turkish force under the personal command of Colonel Kress von Kressenstein, Chief of Staff 8th Corps. Due to a series of unfortunate coincidences the action ended disastrously for A Squadron: only nine men got away. The regiment, in total, suffered 20 dead, 15 wounded and 63 taken prisoner. The survivors of this action were sent back to Kantara shortly afterwards where, in June, they were joined by Lieutenant Wilson with 20 troopers.

On the Briny   7.6.1918
(to Mother)

".....I am writing this just outside the Bay of Biscay .. we are in sight of two or three ships all the time so there is nothing for us to worry about re submarines. We were in sight of the French coast for about an hour yesterday somewhere by Brest and we expect to see the Spanish coast tonight or tomorrow morning.

We didn't sail till 8 o'clock Monday night, we came from Devonport, saw a great many submarines and destroyers, and just as we were leaving, the *Warspite* came in and passed within two hundred yards of us – she was rather badly knocked about but the crew seemed very happy; they were all lined up and cheered like fury when they passed us – it was rather a fine sight.

We have boat drill every morning and we have to keep life belts on all the time. We have just got the news by wireless about the

Hampshire being sunk with Kitchener and his staff. We hope it isn't true, but there are plenty more good men to take his place."

8.6.1918

"...Perfectly lovely today, hardly a ripple on the water, we have been within sight of the Portuguese coast all the morning so hope to get to Gibraltar soon. There was rather a nasty accident on board this morning, eight men were sitting on the hatch of one of the holds and something tipped the whole show over and they all fell about thirty feet. None of them were killed but we are rather anxious about two of them. I am thankful to say none of my chaps were amongst them. There is an electric gymnasium on board where you can ride a bike, camel, ostrich, horse or get a fearful vibration by pressing a button, we have great sport there and it helps to keep us fit. I might not be able to post this at Gib; they don't expect to stop there but may do so now to put the fellows that are hurt off."

'On the Briny'   10.6.1918

"We stayed in Gib. last night but of course were not allowed on shore. We anchored in a harbour behind Gib. and it was a most lovely sight first thing ... we could see, at the same time, orange trees, palm trees, a Spanish bull ring, Spanish cemetery, snow topped mountains at Morocco and some of the fiercest guns you could imagine on the rock itself, besides two or three different types of war-ships.

We have got an escort now and think it will stop with us all the way through the Mediterranean. At present there is no land in sight but we expect to follow the African coast later on – as far as Malta where we are going to get some coal."

"... very rough today, doesn't make much difference to us, but our poor little destroyer, who is escorting is having a very bad time, sometimes we can only just see the top of her mast but the chap still keeps his place in the "Crows nest" I can't think how he manages it! I am Officer of the Watch tonight, have to see that all the sentries are on the alert from 8 till 12. I shall spend most of my time on the Bridge with the Skipper, he is a typical old salt and a very nice old chap, he only joined us at Gib."

Whit-Monday

" ... during my tour of watch we went bang through a terrific thunderstorm – I never saw such lightning. We were in sight of the African coast all the time and, when it lighted up the snow-capped mountains, it was worth walking from England to see."

Sidi Bashra Rest Camp   **18.6.1918**
Alexandria

"Just a line to say I have arrived safely after a delightful voyage – we got into harbour last night about 7.30. We hope to stay here about a fortnight, before joining the Regiment, in order to acclimatise. The heat isn't half bad – people say that today was as hot as they ever get it and none of us was the slightest bit knocked up, although we disembarked and marched up here in the heat of the day. The nights are lovely – just like a May night at home, there is practically no twilight and the sun sets about 6.45.

I left my sword on board and have asked one of the ship's officers to send it to Bish[opstone] so you needn't get the wind up if it arrives ...

This is a lovely camp, 7 miles from town, on the sands. My tent is farthest from the sea and is not more than 20 yards from it at high tide; we bathe nearly all day.

...My own sword had an unusual career. It was a delightful piece of work beautifully engraved, with my own name and Regiment added. When we went to Egypt it was safely tucked into the straps of my valise; the only method of packing a sword. When we landed at Alexandria I was horrified to see my valise come up from the hold without my sword. I made all the fuss I possibly could and some of the ship's officers took quite a serious view of the affair. But it was not found and I had to draw an 'issue' one, just as efficient but lacking the personal touch. Some four months later I received an official notice from from the Harbour-master at Marseilles saying that, when watching divers in the harbour, he had seen one surface with a sword bearing my name and Regiment and what would I like him to do with it. How it had arrived at Marseilles was a complete mystery, we had not touched land anywhere on the voyage out. I imagine some member of our crew had pinched it with a view to selling it when he returned home but, noticing the personalised engraving, decided it would be wiser to throw it overboard. I asked the Harbour-master to send it home and my brother Ted when coming home on leave, quite unaware of the incident, travelled on the same train from Paddington to Shrivenham as my long lost sword.

When I came home I was surprised to find how little damage it had suffered from being so long in salt water and, after a bit of massage and petting, I found that I could still bring the point round to touch the hilt. This was one of my best parlour tricks for years until one day when I was giving a display to four or five people, fortunately on the lawn, it gave a musical twang and flew into a thousand pieces; not large enough to make gramaphone needles, much less ploughshares.

After an eventful journey I reached the Regiment and found them in rather a state of depression. Only a few weeks before my arrival they had lost a complete Squadron except for about seven survivors. The tragedy of losing almost a complete squadron in one morning emphasised the hazards of a Yeomanry Regiment recruited in peace time and then being suddenly hurled into a war. The Regiment was essentially a landlord and tenant affair and each squadron was recruited from a small section of the County. Consequently a disaster of this proportion not only cast a gloom over the Regiment itself but also over the area from which the Squadron originated. A Farmer could lose his son and his landlord in the same battle; anxiety for the family must have been an added burden for brothers fighting side by side. The first man that I saw killed was the youngest of three brothers serving with the Regiment. My own troop not only had two brothers – the Hamlins – but a father and son, the former a farrier, but of course, just as vulnerable as his son, an ordinary Trooper. I must confess that the problem was ever present in my mind but, to their credit, I was never able to detect from their reactions to the occasional 'arrangements' that I made, whether they approved of them or not and they were all excellent soldiers."

Kantara   25.6.1916

"... our general routine is: we get up at 4.30 have a cup of tea and biscuit and go out for about 1½ hours; usually along the Canal bank where we tie our horses together and have a bathe. We then come in an have breakfast at 8 or 8.30, then stables from 9.30-10.30 and finish till noon, when we just water and feed, then we go to sleep until 4 o'clock when we water and feed again. I have a tent to myself and am very comfortable and happy, the other officers are jolly good sports. Lord Apsley is here, a second Lieutenant. There is nothing but sand for miles and miles but we can get from here to Port Said in about half an hour, quite a good train service. We wear shorts (football knickers), shirt and helmet except when riding; we have three horses each and I have got three very good ones, some of them have been out here all the time."

The "threshing machines" are really amusing; they spread the corn around on the ground and hitch a camel or an ox (in one case I saw one of each) on to a flat piece of wood upon which an Arab woman rides and drives round and round till all the corn is knocked out ... I also saw from the train about 30 natives bathing in a dirty little stream and a dead donkey floating gaily past, they didn't take any notice at all ... "

Kantara   **9.7.1916**
(to brother Ted)

"... there are a lot of our airmen here, it is very interesting to see them turn out when an enemy one is reported. The De Haviland, the best of the lot, went after a Fokker about a fortnight ago, just caught him up over the Australians who promptly plugged our man's petrol tank and fetched him down. The Pilots often dine with us and they say they'd sooner fly over Turks than Colonials."

13.7.1916.

" ... I am at the moment of writing sitting outside the Mess hut, waiting for dinner with a magnificent sunset going on behind, a full moon staring me in the face, a drum and pipe band of the Scottish Horse squealing away on my left, the nude figure of Lord Apsley taking a bath on my right, and endless sand all round; that is the situation in Egypt."

Lieutenant Wilson as part of Major Turner's "D" squadron was attached to the Forty-second Division at Pelusium, a position on the newly constructed railway six miles short of Romani, from approximately 20th July.

Pelusium   **20.7.1916**

" ...Just a line to say we have reached our new home after a really enjoyable trek, it took us about 30 hours including a 4 hour rest.

It is much nicer here than where we were, always a lovely breeze and plenty of wood and water for men and horses. I can stand in my tent and touch a huge bunch of dates with a little stick. They will be ripe in about a month; there are tons of them around the camp, the crop of the whole "hod" [grove] is valued at £45,000. We have to destroy [the crop] because if anyone tried to attack the Canal that would be their chief food. It seems an awful waste but can't be helped. I will have my photo taken outside "Date Villa" and send it home...."

Pelusium   **28.7.1916**

"Just another line to say that I'm still quite well and happy. Of course, we don't bubble over with energy in the day time but, at night, we feel like jumping over the moon. I don't know whether I have told you of what our diet chiefly consists of – so here you are:

Breakfast

Porridge
Bacon or Sardines
Eggs all scrambled
Marmalade
Tea or coffee
Flies! (not a few)

Lunch

Cold joint and salad
Fruit
Cheese
Flies!

Tea

Bread and Jam
Cake and biscuits
Tea
Flies!

Dinner

Soup
'Summat 'ot'
Fruit
Sardines on toast
Coffee
No flies (if after 7.30am)

Considering we are at present a detached squadron 30 miles from our HQrs and in the desert, with only a light railway (single line) for communication, this isn't bad. Drink is lime juice invariably.

I have been feeling very important lately, my troop had orders to become attached to the 156th Infantry Brigade, we have been with them about a week. We have to do all their despatch work and occasionally escort a General or two who wants to make a reconnaissance in front of our line ... two days ago we had to show[*] General Lawrence round.

The Brigade staff are a very nice lot, I often have a smoke with them and feel quite the little General myself..."

[*] Major General the Hon. H A Lawrence Commanding Officer No. 3 Section canal defence

Chapter 3

*The battle for Romani which took place in August 1916,
represented both the last concerted enemy offensive against the
Suez Canal and Lieutenant Wilson's 'baptism of fire.' His
descriptions of this campaign illustrate the problems inherent in
desert warfare. There were few tracks and even fewer landmarks;
progress was made by compass readings or, hopefully, following
the man in front. The lack of water was an even greater problem
for the mounted units.*

*According to the official histories the emeny build-up began in
May and, by late July, a combined Turkish and German force of
eighteen thousand occupied a line only thirty miles from and
parallel to the Canal. It stretched from Oghratina near the coast
road to Mageibra some ten miles to the south. The attack was
launched – at German insistence – on August 3rd and although it
failed and Turkish casualties were estimated to be heavy –
probably one third of the total force – the enemy were able to
withdraw to El Arish with the main body of men and all artillery
intact. "D" Squadron, commanded by Major Charles Turner and
in which Lieutenant Wilson was serving, played a significant role
in this battle. At one stage they alone prevented an outflanking
movement by the enemy.*

Hill 70 or Pelusium   10.8.1916

"... We have been hard at it, day and night, since the 4th
(anniversary of declaration of war). We haven't averaged two
hours sleep a night and have often had forty winks when the
lead was flying. We won a great victory the first day at Romani
and got a very impressive wire from the King – perhaps you
saw it in the paper. Since then we have been hunting them out
of the country, which meant about three more lively scraps each
of which I very much enjoyed. Water and heat were the chief
trouble, it meant having thousands of camels following us all the

time with water, am glad to say our men always managed to get some and we have had tea at almost every halt.

My "baptism of fire" didn't have the least effect on me, I hardly knew I was fighting. My squadron held the whole attack for four hours till the rest of our Brigade and some Anzacs turned up, we didn't let them come on an inch and my Squadron Leader was personally thanked by the General, but I will let you have a full account shortly."

Hill 70   16.8.1916

"…We have just returned to camp after our eleven days' campaign. Everything has gone on well and I am just as well and happy as I was two years ago … On August 4th our Squadron was at Pelusium about twenty five miles from the Canal, on the Army railway. The Turks attacked a place called Romani about another seven miles out, which was strongly fortified by us. About nine thousand attacked Romani and two thousand came straight on to Pelusium to cut the railway and water supply. This is the lot our Squadron (one hundred men) met and held till the rest of the Brigade came up, plus a regiment of New Zealanders. Then we drove them right back on to our forts at Romani and any that were alive or unwounded held up a white flag. Our Regiment also captured a battery of guns and we are trying to claim them to put in Gloucester.

It was an awful job getting the prisoners back, we didn't stop fighting till just before dark and had a four and a half hour journey across the Desert after that … this all took place on the first day and we moved out in pursuit the next morning at dawn and found them entrenched at Qatia. This is a palm grove with a high ridge behind it, and another low ridge just in front of it and then about three miles of level sand. It was here that I spent the most exciting moments of my life. It was impossible for Infantry to cross the plain so they said we had to go – that was our

48

Brigade and three Anzac Brigades – what a sight! We all extended over about three and a half miles and started quietly off for the low ridge, the only cover to be seen, and only just high enough to hide the horses. At that shells began to arrive but we didn't break out of a walk – as we wanted to do a bit of a burst at the finish – and when we got about half a mile off we started off at the gallop. Bullets and shrapnel seemed to be everywhere and we were all very glad to reach the ridge. Well, there we stopped for about five hours and couldn't go any further. Then the order came to retire a troop at a time which took about two hours and that looked like being worse than coming. However, we managed to get back again alright; I was the last officer in our Brigade to leave the position. We went out again next morning but Johnny Turk had gone, and we have been after him up until the 12th, when we left him to take a trip of 49 miles, over waterless desert, back home.

The Turks are good sports, one day a Taube flew over and dropped a message saying "Please mark your hospitals more distinctly," three days afterwards they came and dropped about 25 bombs – at one place we found a message "Good fight, don't drive us too hard, your cavalry has beaten us" and, "Don't stop here long it is infected with cholera," so we cleared out. They are not very pleased with the German officers; we put the prisoners in a barbed wire compound and they refused to be with the Germans, and threw them out through the wire. They say they will never attack again – just fifty per cent of their force are casualties, they spent three days burning their stores and they've got no money, so we hope to take it easy a bit. We lived on "bully and biscuits," which was brought up on camels, also a good supply of water."

Several unusual, and often amusing incidents happened during my "baptism of fire" in the desert. I was lying close to a very dour Welshman, Sergeant Humphries, when a bullet hit a cloud of sand up about three yards in front of us. It continued to

49

journey beneath the sand and just had force enough to appear very slowly out of the sand and come to a halt within an inch of Sergeant Humphries' nose. He just glanced at it and pushed it back into the sand with his forefinger saying, "That's that place for you, little fellow."

On that day fighting ceased as it got dark and the Regiment had to go back to Railhead to water the horses, but I was told to remain with a captured Turkish doctor who still had some wounded to attend. By the time I had delivered the Turkish doctor to HQ, made sure he had something to eat and drink and attended to my horse, there was not much time for sleep. After tying my horse to the lines, I lay down, completely exhausted, and dropped off at once – to be awakened almost immediately by a horse putting his foot plumb in the middle of my chest. I sat up, just in time to be knocked flat again by his hind foot hitting me a hefty blow on the forehead. I looked up to see an Australian, fast asleep in the saddle, his horse aimlessly drifting about among sleeping soldiers but I couldn't bother to do anything about it. It seemed only a matter of minutes before I realised that the war was about to be resumed. I could hear Major Charles Turner carrying on that two or three of his officers were casualties and, knowing that I had been left behind the night before, probably never expected to see me again. He ended his tale of woe by saying "… and if I ever find that bloody Wilson again there's sure to be something the matter with him." I think he felt flattered when I proved him right by sitting up and revealing a copy of a horse shoe, in bright red, imprinted on my chest – every nail of which could be counted – and the shape of a hind hoof in black and blue all over my forehead. He just said "What are you going to do?" "Coming along with you, Sir," and off we went in pursuit of the poor old routed Turk.

Their wounded, sick and exhausted, were dotted about all over the desert. Their comrades had done what they could to provide a bit of shade and they all had water but it was too brackish to drink. They had evidently been told what to do when we came along and, without exception, insisted on shaking hands, some smiling merrily and some pointing to a wound or pain and closing their eyes as if to tell us they had not long to live. We did what we could for them in the way of cigarettes, or a drink of our rather better water and robbed our signallers of some flags to show our RAMC people where they were.

On a third sleepless night we were going back for water and the Turks were following us. My troop was last in the column and practically every man was sound asleep in the saddle. On these night marches I assumed a sense of responsibility foreign to my normal standards and, whenever the column came to halt, I would slip off my horse and stand about 20 yards on one side. It was so easy for them to move off again with no warning and the column would be broken. That is exactly what happened although I was straining my eyes and listening for any sound of movement. The troop in front of mine suddenly came to life and completely disappeared into the blue before I could get on to my horse again. I hadn't a clue in which direction they had gone and this was in the sandy desert. There was only one thing to do – stay put till daylight. We did the normal thing under the circumstances, formed all the horses in to a circle with their heads in the centre, pulled the reins over their heads and threaded a surcingle through every rein. I told the troop to lie down behind their horses with their rifles in their hands, and I did a lone sentry duty all night on top of a little sand dune. Sergeant Stock and one or two men offered to relieve me but I felt personally responsible for the predicament in which we found ourselves and preferred to see it through. We heard the Turk once or twice but were not worried unduly, as I did not suppose he knew where we were any more than I did. We were able to track the Regiment in the sandy desert at dawn and safely joined up with them after about two hours. No one thought it necessary to give me a reprimand, and I don't think the affair was ever mentioned – perhaps no one knew we had been missing all night.

We had been standing to all night and the cooks had just brewed up some porridge at dawn when the shooting started. Jack Taylor, my groom, always had an eye out for food either for himself or our three horses so when he had got me safely mounted, he dashed across to the dixies and crammed his mess-tin with this half-cooked, uninviting, stodgy rubbish. His job when we were dismounted in action was to hold my horse, the spare, and his own. All the horses were safely tucked away behind a sand dune from which we were firing. The Turks had begun to show signs of uneasiness and Major Turner – who incidentally got his DSO in this scrap – thought they were ripe for "galloping" ("galloping" was almost a religion with him). "Get mounted," he shouted, "And get ready to charge." We all scrambled down the sand dune and Jack was trying to swallow some of his porridge and hold onto the three horses at the same time. I just had time to say "Buck up, Jack, I think we are going to charge" before 'phut,' and I knew that some man or horse had been hit. Jack evidently agreed as he was looking at me with the same concern as I was regarding him. Suddenly he yelled "God a'mighty, I been hit, somebody come and take care o' me boss's 'osses. I'm off!" Fortunately he was back in about a month and remained with me until the end of the war.

Hill 70   20.8.1916
(to Lawes [cousin?])

"...we were fighting with the Anzacs cavalry all the time – they are marvellous fellows, but very slow – we left them standing once when we had orders to take a hill where a battery of guns were; we had collared guns and all by the time they got there. The guns are going to be given to the Regiment and put in Gloucester Square if we can get them home. The gunners put up a good show and fired point blank at us till we got within 200 yards of them, when most of them joined the majority!"

"...Am glad to say we are all well and happy, no sickness of any sort to speak of after the rough 'doos.' I noticed in a cutting from *The Times* that the Glosters and Warwicks moved forward as steady as on parade; that wasn't any credit to us, as we were all very anxious to move a lot faster to get under cover."

Chapter 4

After the battle of Romani the Regiment returned to Hill 70, a fortified position on the railway only a few miles from the Canal, and remained there until late September. Lt Wilson spent the first three weeks of September on a course in Cairo. As soon as he rejoined the Regiment, still at Hill 70, he was sent with his troop to Bally Bunion some six miles distant. They caught up with the main force at Nabit on October 3rd and stayed there until early November carrying out reconnaissance patrols into the desert and continuing with general training. During November camp was moved several times and at the end of the month the Regiment was sent back to Dueidar, a rest area ten miles east of Kantara.

After the battle of Romani the Regiment returned to Hill 70, a fortified position on the railway only a few miles from the Canal, and remained there until late September. Lieutenant Wilson meantime, was sent to Cairo for a "refresher" course, rejoining the Regiment about a week before it moved twenty miles forward to Nabit on 29th September. They stayed there until November carrying out reconnaissance patrols into the desert. Camp was moved several times during November – at one stage back to a rest area at Dueidar only ten miles from Kantara – otherwise continuing with outpost duties and general training.

In December the troops were moved eastward to continue the offensive; this time the plan was to take El Arish, the next town of importance along the coast. In the event the Turkish forces evacuated it before any attack could take place and Christmas was spent peaceably enough at a village called Mullah, west of El Arish.

Reorganisation of the EEF in January put the Gloucester Hussars into the 5th Mounted Brigade, Imperial Mounted Division, a part of Lieutenant General Sir Philip Chetwode's Desert Column. They then took a major role in the cavalry raid on

Rafa, a town held by an estimated two thousand Turks and on the frontier with Palestine. Lieutenant Wilson was shot in the arm whilst acting as 'galloper' to the Brigadier.

Grand Continental Hotel, Cairo   16.9.1916

"...you will never go inside the Pyramids for the simple reason that you have to crawl down a sort of rabbit hole about 100 yards long and 3½ feet high with a most awful stuffy sort of smell – covered in all sorts of insects, beetles, etc. and without exaggeration, in one place especially, there was a huge bat-mouse hanging from the ceiling every two yards. The natives of course behave in the most religious manner (you have to employ two each, one to carry a candle, and the other to grovel about at your feet to prevent you slipping as the floor is greasy). At the end of the passage you come into a high sort of chamber (not enamel) which contains the tombs – we happened to be a bit of a musical party so we gave 'em *Come Landlord fill the flowing bowl* – it echoed all round and sounded topping. This so impressed the natives they nearly all sort of cried and stood with their mouths open – so, in order to 'relieve the pressure,' we switched on to *We'll all go hunting today."*

Bally-Bunion   26.9.1916

"...I am at a place called Bally-Bunion (some name) with just my troop of thirty-four men, on my own. I send out patrols every day and wait here until they come back at night. There is a Battery of Artillery here and I mess with the Artillery, only three officers, and we have quite a good time. I am about six miles from the Regiment and keep having to talk to some of them over the phone which is just outside my tent. The men love it here, they are living in comparative luxury as there was a Brigade of Australians here before we came and they never think of taking anything away with them. Consequently the place is full of beds, chairs, tables, etc. and all the tents are furnished as per "Waring & Gillow."

My *special* furniture up to date is a 'wash stand' with a cupboard underneath – quite a good 'table-come-desk' affair and an easy chair which contains two little cupboards – of course they are all made from empty cartridge boxes, etc but are quite up to the occasion. The only work the patrols do is to take my mess-tin out and bring it back full of dates every night."

Nabit   **19.10.1916**

"...Major Turner (my Squadron Leader) has been given the DSO for that affair on Aug 4th. I thought he would – another chap, Lt Mitchell from Tatbury, has the MC and two Sgts, DCMS ... glad my sword has turned up; it has probably had more of a history than if it had stuck to me....

Nabit   **22.10.1916**
(to brother Ted)

"... we are taking things very easy now, doing nothing but patrols – some of these last about 50 or 60 hours and are very interesting. We take camels with us to carry Dixies and grub and have a jolly good time as a rule. The sleeping part is the worst of it as the nights are cold and we get very heavy dews but we generally sit awake and smoke or eat at night, and have a nap in the heat of the day and a good sleep when we get back.

We get some first class singing here out of the Welsh Squadron; they form a lovely choir of about 30, we have a Cathedral alto – the best voice I think I have ever heard. Sundays we have a voluntary church parade at night – the chaplain rides over – and he lets them choose their own hymns and they "carry on" with hymns, chants and Anthems for an hour or two after the service. Nearly every week night they sing part songs, finishing every time with the departure (their star turn)..."

Nabit   **3.11.1916**
(to brother Jack)

"...We are still in the same place and doing nothing but patrols and escorts. Yesterday I had to ride down to the railway to bring some money to the Regiment, had about £400 on the saddle nearly all silver.

When I was on a three day Trek with my troop last month, the advanced guard drove three gazelles (a sort of deer a bit bigger than a sheep) within fifteen yards of me – they came round a hill and stopped short. I tried to get my revolver out but was too late – two or three fellows got off but they were out of sight before they could shoot – they would have been a prize asset to us just then.

...There are plenty of vultures here, they hover over camel convoys for hours – camels peg out very easily, they are very delicate – its nothing to pass twenty or thirty a day, they don't half 'Oliver Cromwell'."

25.11.1916.

"... We start for our Rest tomorrow DV* the trek will probably take us five or six days so if you don't hear for a bit, you'll understand.

We captured an Arab last night to finish up the patrol, we've sent him to Brigade Headquarters today. They are as cunning as Monkeys – some of them rode up to an Anzac camp about two miles from us the other night and one got his camel shot. The Anzacs sent and asked us to send out a patrol to try and catch him – so we sent out a Corporal and six men – they were out all night but couldn't see him. But during the Corporal's

* Deo Volente (God Willing)

absence he had walked into our camp, gone to the same Corporal's hut and pinched his water bottle and a loaf of bread. We could track his bare foot marks in the morning but never caught him. We tied the one up with about thirty yards of rope last night and put his feet in sacks to keep him quite safe. We ought to have a most enjoyable trek; we are going to make for the railway and then follow it back so we shall be close to water and grub all the time."

Mallah   24.12.1916

"... At last I have time to write a bit of news. Since I last wrote a lot has taken place – our rest was abruptly cut short. The Turks had got to El Arish which you will probably see on a Bible map on the coast and had made about six miles of trenches. About 30,000 Infantry, four Anzac Brigades and our Brigade were rushed up to drive them out. We finished the journey by trekking all night and got into a position just before dawn. As soon as it got light we peeped over a hill and there were these Turkish trenches but no sign of Johnny Turk. I was sent out with my troop to see if there was anything about and rode slowly along their trenches and called on the dug-outs but no one was at home – they had all cleared out in the night. We halted there and the Anzacs went on another ten miles but didn't catch them up so they are probably in Palestine by now. We have come back again and are taking it easy; we must have trekked nearly 180 miles and had to come back again because they couldn't keep us supplied ... Our horses stood up very well – some of them didn't have more than a quart of water for three days and about one third of their proper rations. I had a bit of sport on the evening before we started for the night journey. All the men's water bottles were empty and only the Anzacs had a supply place there and said they couldn't supply us. So I got about forty men and took every bottle in the Regiment, about 400 and went over to the supply stores and started to argue round the taps with the officer in charge. In the meantime I sent

59

the men round to the top of the tanks and before we had come to any arrangement the bottles were full and we were marching back again. It was very dark so no one was upset about it."

The Battle of Rafa took the course of a cavalry raid and was undertaken by Lieutenant General Sir Philip Chetwode – later Field Marshal Lord Chetwode – a cavalry leader of the old school. The force consisted of our Brigade, the Fifth Mounted, the Anzac Mounted Division, the Imperial Camel Corps and a battery of the HAC*. We had twenty-nine miles of desert to ride and had to be ready to rush the position, if possible, at dawn. However the Turks and Germans were expecting us and heavy fighting broke out as soon as it was light enough to see. I had been detailed as galloper to the Brigadier and my troop was taken over by the excellent Sergeant Stock. I was always miserable when I was detached from my troop and, although this sort of job could be very interesting, I was always worried that something might go wrong with them.

The battle was proceeding when I was told to take a message to the Commanding Officer of the Warwickshire Yeomanry who were in action about half a mile to our right. I left Jack Taylor with my spare horse safely tucked behind a sand dune, galloped across, handed my horse to one of the Warwickshire horse-holders, and started to run up to the ridge where they were heavily engaged. Suddenly I thought I had been blown to smithereens, something hit me with such terrific force that, although I was running forward as fast as I could, I did a complete somersault backwards. I sat where I was and the Sergeant in charge of the led horses called out "Bad Luck, Sir, where have you got it?" "Damned if I know" I replied, "All over the place I think." Then I saw a little trickle of blood running down my arm and realised that I had the simplest of wounds: a bullet through the top of my arm. But it must have touched a nerve or something to give me such a shock. I hung about, did a few more messages for an hour or two, and was then told to

* Honourable Artillery Company

take the wounded of the Brigade back to where we had come from – in other words – to ride the twenty-nine miles of desert again.

When I got back to the casualties I was grieved to see an officer of the Warwicks, a man called Jack Ware with whom I had soldiered at Tidworth, among the dead. He had been hit exactly between the eyebrows. With some difficulty we managed to get the wounded on their horses and started our journey. By this time I was not feeling too well and told the party that I intended to do the journey without a halt, as some of the men were weakening rapidly and I feared we should never get them on their horses again if I let them dismount. We had done about fifteen miles when I noticed two horsemen approaching and, when we met, I could see that it was a Medical Officer and his orderly. The officer was immaculately dressed, very officious and evidently, very new. He rode up to me and said "Have you all been inoculated for tetanus?" I had to say that none of us had been. "Every man dismount," he ordered. I tried to point out to him that some of the men were in bad shape and that I was on my way to an Australian Field Hospital which I hoped to reach in three or four hours and where we could all be inoculated. But he insisted, so we all lay on our backs, opened our shirts, and he stuck a needle into our midriffs as big as a hydraulic drill.

His orderly was filling the thing up for him and was not paying much attention to the doctor's horse, which slowly started wandering in the direction from which it had come. One of the men, not in my Regiment said, "It's all right Sir, I'll catch him for you," and started off in pursuit. He didn't seem to be in much of a hurry and I put it down to the effects of his wound when he allowed the doctor's horse to go over the first sand dune. When the doctor had finished his inoculations there was still no sign of his horse and the rest of us resumed our journey. Every now and again I caught sight of a man with a 'led' horse going over sand dunes and thought he must have gone delirious. After about six miles we came across him sitting on the sand with a grin all over his face. "This is just what I wanted for my Officer; a lovely chestnut mare, saddle wallets full of fags and grub, saddle bags full of drink, and all on a brand new officer's saddle." She was indeed a beautiful mare in tip-top condition and I felt very badly about it but, by then, there was nothing I could do. I had to give him full marks for having his Officer's welfare at heart despite his own fairly serious wound.

With difficulty we found the Australian Field Hospital at about 3am. It consisted of one marquee and six bell tents and there was no sign of life. After knocking on the tents, a great bearded Australian poked his head out and said, "What in Hell's the matter?" I told him I had a bunch of wounded. I knew that they had been warned to expect some casualties but didn't say so as I needed all the help they could offer. Eventually a few more Anzacs appeared, attended to our horses and we were shown into tents. My bearded friend took me to a tent with one bed in it, with white sheets, and handed me some pyjamas. He never asked me what was the matter but gave me a bottle of port and said, "Get that inside you Digger, and you'll be all right in the morning" which was quite true. I woke about 6am and looked out of my tent, just in time to see the rest of the troops returning. Nearly every other man was asleep in the saddle and, as I watched, I saw Major Tommy Longworth, Commander of 'C' Squadron detach himself from the column and ride towards me and, just when I was going to welcome him, I saw that he was fast asleep and, unconsciously, putting a bit of tight rein on. The Artillery were marching parallel with the Regiment but on the other side of the hospital. His horse joined up with them and continued back to camp with the gunners! I often wondered what the major felt when he found out what happened.

The raid was a complete success. Our casualties were not too heavy but among those who were killed was poor old Corporal Wiltshire who started off from Tidworth with me – his mess-tin around his neck. Among the prisoners was a German Major who was in charge of their machine guns, a magnificent, well-dressed figure. I said, "Good morning," to him and he replied in perfect English "Good morning to you – wasn't that a damned good scrap?" He had been at Oxford for three years just before war broke out.

I felt rather guilty when we were told to get ready to go back to Railhead where we should find a hospital train to take us to Port Said.* I felt perfectly fit; my arm was slightly stiff but the injection we had been given made us all feel a bit groggy. Judging by the size of his syringe I imagine the poor un-horsed doctor had pumped about ten times the proper dose into us. The idea of a fortnight in hospital was, to say the least, very tempting as we had been living under the stars for many months without a sight of civilisation and were sadly in need of a clean-up. Nevertheless I think if I could have found a horse saddled up I should have jumped on him and gone in search of the Regiment.

* They were actually sent by train to Kantara, then by boat to Port Said

Chapter 5

Lieutenant Wilson was initially sent to hospital at Port Said where he made the most of any opportunity offered for diversion. At the end of January he was sent to Alexandria to convalesce and in mid-February – after a few days' leave at Corps HQ at Kantara on the Canal – he caught up with the Regiment at El Burg, a settlement about ten miles further up the coast from El Arish.

From this point he participated in the patrols sent forward to protect the water pipelines, railway and wire roads under construction by British engineers and the wells at Sheik Zowaiid

By March 1917 the troops had moved up-coast to the frontier with Palestine at Rafa, preliminary to the planned assault on Gaza. Known as the "Gateway to Palestine" Gaza, with its large population and command of trade routes to the interior, was garrisoned by a sizeable Turkish force. The intention was to neutralise this force and prevent its withdrawl northward.

The operation began on March 26th and the Gloucester Hussars were engaged on the left flank, part of a group intended to divert enemy troops from the main attack. Lieutenant Wilson's troop went ahead some distance by themselves and he lost a sergeant and corporal in the action.

The first battle for Gaza failed, due – it is said – to poor planning as much as the fog which delayed the initial advance for a crucial two hours. The Regiment moved back to Deir-el-Belah to prepare for a further attack, scheduled for 17th April. This, too, proved to be an expensive failure and Allied casualties were three times that of the enemy.

31st General Hospital, Port Said
(to brother Jack)

"… we are very happy and comfortable here and enjoy ourselves very much – quite an interesting bunch of patients. Last night we had a dressing-gown lecture on the navigation of the worst straits of the Pacific Islands; it would have been very clear only the old Skipper that was lecturing had had too much Scotch.

There are also a lot of Russian Officers here who were sunk by torpedo just outside Port Said; they can speak English and are very interesting.

I'm practically all right now and find nothing at all [wrong with] my arm. It was a clean wound right through the flesh of the right arm – just above the elbow – the pain was nothing. It seemed just as if someone had hit it with a sledge hammer and then it seemed to weigh a ton. I was surprised with the force of the blow – it knocked me head over tip…"

22.1.1917.

31st General Hospital, Port Said

"… I can't tell that my arm was ever bad now – I feel absolutely nothing of it – and wouldn't have missed it for £20. We had a good entertainment on Sunday. A Russian officer is in the next bed to me – I was having forth winks on my bed in a very 'undress' costume, when a troop of Russian priests filed in and went through a grand performance – they had the most ridiculous costumes I ever saw and long hair done up in a bun '*a la* Madam Baldwin' at the back. I nearly busted myself to keep from laughing but had to crawl away to have a good laugh. I shouldn't have laughed I don't think, only I caught the Russian's eye, who also saw the joke and that did it. Nearly all the Russians speak English and are very interesting to talk to."

27.1.1917.

"...The Sisters and Doctors are giving us a concert in the town tonight and DV, we are all going, it will make a nice change even if it isn't much good.

Our Brigade had a very nice message from General Fitzgerald (Inspector General of Cavalry) who was at Rafa and watched our attack – he sympathised with us over our casualties and said a Brigade of British Guards wouldn't have taken the position before midnight even if they attempted it, and he thought that was doubtful."

28.1.1917.

"...The concert was quite a success and, strange to say, they did the same sketch as Betty's crowd at Shrivenham. One of the Sisters used to be an actress and she got up quite a useful scene affair. "Belgium" is lying on the stage half dead wih her flag by her side and Britannia comes on and sees her and then calls in all the Colonies and Allies and sings "a few kind words" about each. They then form up and in comes Germany and all that crowd amidst shrieks and bangs, when "peace" comes along and stops the noise. Germany etc., kneel down, France picks up Belgium and Britannia returns her flag and then they all go home to tea. It was really done well and the costumes were splendid."

The hospital at Port Said was housed in a vast canal building and, unfortunately, the canal separated us from the 'city of sin' as it has been called. We were not allowed out of the hospital of course, but three of us contrived to make it across every night, although it proved to be very expensive. We had a good dinner at the Eastern Exchange Hotel and, as that was also the haunt of the doctors and nurses, we had to eat in a private room for which we were charged nearly double the price. The most annoying thing was the cost of crossing the Canal. Some wicked old dago would cheerfully row us across for five piastres – about a shilling – but when we stealthily crept down to the little pier on our return, sometimes after midnight, he would lay off about five or ten yards until we had collected a hundred piastres – a pound – tied it in a handkerchief and thrown it to him. We could not argue for too long as there was always a risk of doctors and nurses arriving.

In ten days, officially suffering from 'gun shot wound', I spent over £72 which was six months pay for a subaltern. One night it was nearly 3 o'clock before we could get back. We had been warned that a vey strict Night Sister – or some rank of that sort – would be visiting the ward during the night and that, if we were discovered, there would be real trouble. Forewarned is to be forearmed; I armed myself with a bottle of champagne. We peeped into the little glass-partitioned office of the otherwise darkened ward of nearly a hundred beds and, sure enough, the Dragon was there in earnest conversation with the Ward Sister and two nurses. That was enough to tell us that the cat was out of the bag. We went into conference and decided to take our boots off and, while I gave myself up, the other two would take advantage of the diversion and make a dash for their beds. I removed the wire from the bottle before I crept in but could not restrain the cork long enough to reach the office; the wretched thing went off like a cannon and woke every single patient when I was still a few yards from the office door. By that time I was beyond caring – I rushed in and said, "Glasses Matron, quickly!" Whether it was due to fright or shock at being given a short sharp shock for once, I shall never know but four glasses reached the top of the bottle in a matter of seconds. They enjoyed the party and all was well.

Whilst in hospital and longing for a bit of shooting, I made enquiries of the old man who came round with the papers. After a couple of days he told me that everything had been arranged. That was one outstanding characteristic of even the lowest grade of 'street Arab': they could 'arrange' anything. I had to be at the station at 7.30am where I should meet a guide with gun and cartridges, prepared for a days' shooting. I had to do my own 'arranging' with some of the other patients so that, when I was wanted by a nurse or doctor, they would be told that I was having a bath.

I have no idea where I spent this days' shooting* except that, after about two hours on the train, we alighted at a station by the Nile the name of which I distinctly remember was Tanta. The old guide had made his plans and a boat was waiting for us. After paddling about for a while a huge bird came flopping along overhead and in terrific excitement the guide shouted "Wild goose!" I knew it was only a sheldrake and useless for cooking, but to satisfy him, I had a crack at it and killed it. He was overjoyed at his prize of a "wild goose" or at the thought that I knew no better!

He had told me beforehand that he had also 'arranged' for some wonderful pigeon shooting in the afternoon and, after a while, we landed and walked about two miles over some intensively irrigated land until we arrived at a small mud-hut village where I was introduced to the headman. A chair was already placed in the square formed by the little houses and, after being given some coffee, I was led to the chair. Then the lads of the village started running round the houses beating sticks and soon the air was full of their tame pigeons. I hesitated to shoot at them but was urged on by everyone. The guide said that it was the time for killing them and it would save them the expense and trouble of doing it themselves. So I

* Tanta is some 100m SW of Port Said

started blazing away and, I must admit, it was very good fun. I had one cartridge left when I decided to call it a day – which proved to be fortunate. I gave the headman a £1 note as arranged, and after more coffee and much hand-shaking, started back to the station.

I soon became aware of a howling shrieking mob of blue-gowned natives running after us. This was alarming enough, but when I noticed my guide going 'hell for leather' ahead of me I sensed real danger. I would not run, but put my remaining cartridge in the gun and walked slowly on. They soon caught up with me and were like a pack of hungry hounds – all yelling "buckshee, buckshee!" I tried to make them understand that I had paid the agreed sum to the headman, but to no avail. All the while I was jumping over irrigation streams and luckily, for some unknown reason, none of them ever got in front of me. There must have been more than fifty of them but they kept at my heels all the time.

Eventually we arrived at the main stream which was at least twenty feet wide with a single plank to serve as a bridge. I was never good at crossing streams by plank under the best of conditions and was particularly anxious not to make a mistake on this occasion – for I am certain that the bottom of that stream had been decided on as my last resting place.

As I stepped off the plank on to *terra firma* the most villainous looking creature I have ever seen landed by my side. He was a foot taller than I was – I am over six feet – and had taken the twenty foot stream in his stride. As he landed he raised his right arm and there emerged from his sleeve a dagger with a huge blade and its point was within an inch of my throat. Instinctively I struck the muzzle of my gun within an inch of his chin and there we stood, for what seemed a fortnight but was certainly minutes, I didn't feel brave until he started to shuffle backwards, found the bridge and retreated across it, still staring at me and holding the knife in the same threatening manner.

I have since realised how foolish it was to take such a risk. Only two people knew I was out of the hospital, no one but the guide knew where I had gone, and any one of those rascals would have murdered me for my boots. Nothing could have been easier than to cut my throat and kick me into the stream and I should never have been heard of again.

We were surprised a few days later to hear that all the wounded would be going to a private convalescent home in Alexandria. This was run by a charming New Zealand couple and was sheer luxury – with practically no rules or regulations. I felt a fraud but thoroughly enjoyed the rest of our escapades at Port Said. Nevertheless much as I enjoyed this peaceful interlude, I was glad when the time came to go up to the line again. I hated being away from my troop and always feared that some of my unscrupulous pals would pinch my horses.

8.2.1917

British Red Cross Convalescent Hospital No. 10
Ibrahimieh Alexandria

"... I leave here tomorrow and go to our base where I shall probably be for a week or two before I go to the Regt. The base is at Kantara and the Regt. over 130 miles from there...

It is rather a sad coincidence but nearly every member of our Welsh Choir was either killed or wounded on the 9th (at Rafa)..."

El Burg   10.3.1917

"... We are moving about 10 miles further up tomorrow, we have looked out a lovely camp right on the beach – with plenty of good water close by.

General Chetwode our CIC has arranged for a big race meeting there between the two Cavalry Divisions and it promises to be a great day. We are going to have a "Paddock" and several side shows ... the missing link will be the Ascot fashions.

I received a lovely parcel of mince pies and cakes yesterday, thank you very much indeed, they arrived in splendid condition and nothing could have been more acceptable...

The Turks have gone right back to Jerusalem now – at least, that is the latest information – and we expect to get into Palestine a bit, and then sit down. I don't think the French want us to invade Palestine."

Soon after I rejoined the Regiment my troop was doing advanced guard for the Brigade over new territory. We were the first British troops to reach the area and were well fanned out covering a wide front, as the country was pure desert. I had been without tobacco for three to four days, which was very irksome. There was little hope of any mail from home reaching us for many days as we were advancing faster than the supply column which usually brought up any mail. I saw my Sergeant dismount and pick something up. Then he galloped across to me, produced a 2oz tin of tobacco, and said it was of no use to him. This was indeed more than a coincidence, I regarded it as a miracle. The explanation came later. The Turks had raided an Australian camp while most of the regiment were out on a big reconnaissance. They overran the few men remaining in the lines, looted their canteen, including all their tobacco, and some careless Turk must have dropped a tin for me.

Sheik Zowaiid   **12.3.1917**
(to brother Jack)

"...Yesterday three or four of us had a ride over the Rafa battlefield, it was very interesting but presented a rather dreary sight. They'd got a wonderful position and if we'd seen it before we shouldn't have been quite so keen to get there. I also had a good look into Palestine, in fact I was only about four hundred yards from the frontier, but we had no time to go any further.

We have just heard that Bagdad* has fallen – that will probably force the Turks to retire further on this front – the general opinion is that fighting is finished as far as we are concerned.

…we've had a terrible sand storm that lasted three days and nights – we had built a lovely Mess but first it blew the roof and sides away and then buried the table and seat and we don't know within twenty yards where it is now. I suppose the next Regiment will find it and put it down as Pharaoh's pantry."

Rafa   **25.3.1917**

"… we are camping just on the frontier line now and yesterday we started at 4am and made reconnaissance into Palestine of about twenty-six miles. It is a delightful country, cultivated to perfection and the crops look quite good if not better than most English farms, chiefly barley and wheat. The villages were very pretty – a mass of Orange, Fig and other fruit trees – we bought hundreds of Jaffa oranges off the natives, the sheep and cattle were also quite passable. The relief of seeing such country after the miles and miles of bare sand was worth five years of a life."

In action   **2.4.1917**

"… We did an outpost in a garden the other night and captured about half an acre of spring onions and we've been living on biscuits, cheese and onions every since. We went to a farm the other night to buy some eggs, but were told to come back next morning as they would lay at sunrise. So we turned up, but the poor old chap was in an awful way because some

* Bagdad was captured by forces under General Sir Stanley Maude 11th March 1917

Australians had come with a bayonet and topped all the fowls' heads off, and left them laying in rows under their perches."

8.4.1917

"... Our Brigade is going back for a rest in a day or two, I think – and we shall be very glad of it – during the last fortnight we have only carried one blanket and a toothbrush to save the weight, not a razor in the Regiment, you never saw such a lot of tramps in your life. We managed to get hold of our stuff yesterday however and had a good clean-up, and slept like tops.

Morgan and I had an exciting time during the first day of the Gaza battle. The Regiment was attacking a redoubt which was about nine hundred yards away and the Commanding Officer said Morgan's troop was going to advance to a ridge about fifty yards in front, and, when he got there, my troop was to go up on his right. Off went Morgan like the wind, and when he got to the ridge off went my little lot. But Morgan didn't stop and was just disappearing over the ridge in front of the ridge he was supposed to stop on, so I followed.

Eventually after going about five hundred yards (and over four or five nasty little hills) he stopped – no one else followed or we could have taken it easily – but our two troops only numbered about twenty and to make matters more complicated the Infantry, who were over on our right, retired – and at the same time as we got two orders: one – to retire at once, and another – that we were to stop there till dark as it wasn't safe to retire. So we effected a compromise and fired all our ammunition and quietly walked back. I couldn't help laughing at Morgan – if it hadn't been for shortness of wind I don't think he would have stopped this side of Jerusalem."

I was suffering from sunstroke following a nasty little encounter with the enemy which had lasted until dawn, and then a murderous twenty mile trek back to water the horses. By that time I was completely out on my feet and I can just remember the MO telling Jack Taylor to take me to the field ambulance, about another five miles of desert away. Another trooper came with us to hold me up in the saddle. When we reached the dressing station I asked them to leave me. All I wanted to do was to apply the usual tourniquet to my temples and try to get some sleep. This was about 2 o'clock in the morning and, when I awoke at dawn I found I was separated from the hospital by about two hundred parked camels.

An Australian orderly spotted me and came over with a cup of hot cocoa which put new life into me. He was promptly followed by a sizeable bunch of German bombers which suddenly appeared out of the rising sun and blew the poor camels to pieces. The outside of a camel is bad enough but, when you probe deeper, you reach the depths of beastliness! I decided that this was no place for me and, feeling better, started looking round for a horse – anybody's horse. About half a mile away I saw a horseman, mounted in a most unorthodox manner. He was standing in one stirrup on one side of his horse and not moving. He told me later that he had been 'standing by' for a while in case the Huns came back. As I approached I was delighted to recognise a man from the Regiment. He was surely a hospital case; he had a carbuncle – big as a cricket ball and the same colour – on that part of the anatomy used for sitting in the saddle. His breeches had been removed and he looked a very sorry sight. I felt justified in taking his horse and found the Regiment as they were returning to battle. I was happy to be with them again despite the usual grins and jibes from my comrades.

Deir-el-Belah   16.4.1917

"... We are still in the same camp, just like being at Bournemouth except that we don't have to be so particular about our dress. Miss West* would like the life all right because of the tea we get – its astonishing what we drink – we have a cup before stables in the morning, then breakfast – then lunch, then for tea, and again for supper. When we are in camp we keep the Dixies going nearly all the time. I expect we are better off than a lot of people at home as regards living, we always get a full ration of jolly good meat and two vegetables – one of which is always potatoes – jam, tea, sugar, tinned milk, bacon, porridge and cheese and a loaf of bread per man a day; each man gets fifty cigarettes and two ounces of bacca a week, and about twice a week an issue of figs or raisins."

At midnight April 17th the Royal Gloucester Hussars as part of the 5th Mounted Brigade left Deir-el-Belah to take part in the second battle for Gaza. They proceeded along the Wadi el Sharia to Khirbet Um Rijl (see Map †) and they were engaged in that sector until relieved by the Bucks Yeomanry. They withdrew to Tel-el-Jemmi and stayed in reserve until the 19th when they took part in the attack against the Turkish strong point known as Sausage Hill and situated to the right of Wadi Baha. After a heavy counter attack by Turkish forces the Brigade was forced to disengage and a general counter attack was ordered on the evening of 20th April. The regiment was constantly on the move during this period and for the rest of April and May. Lt. Wilson's letters, particularly that of 8th May to his brother Jack, illustrate far more than official records the apparent lack of communication and general confusion. The "dismounted attack" he refers to is that along the Wadi Baha on 19th April.

* Presumably a tea-drinking lady in Bishopstone
† Page 82

Beni-Salah or Tel-el-Marakeb   8.5.1917
(to brother Jack)

"...We have been very busy with the Turks lately and had one very stiff day when the two Cavalry Divisions made a dismounted attack up a valley of about four miles. Our Division did all that was asked but we couldn't make quite a job of it as the other Division couldn't clear the right bank of the valley we were in and, naturally, we were [at that time] enfiladed "pretty nicely." So we had to hang on until after dark when the horses were rushed up and we cleared out. You never saw such a muddle in your life, thousands of horses walking about in all directions with one man to about five (when held by anyone at all) but we all managed to get away all right. I was left with six men in a dry river bed as a sort of rear guard to our Regiment who were [retiring] down it and a sniper kept crawling towards us and shooting about every two minutes, but he evidently couldn't see us – neither could we see him – as he was in some standing Barley (one is allowed to walk standing Barley when shooting in Palestine!).When time was up for me to clear out, we let about thirty rounds supplemented by a small contribution from my revolver, into where we thought he was, he wasn't very many yards away and I'll bet it put the wind up him properly.

During the day the Turks made two or three good counter-attacks, they came on like good sportsmen firing from the hips, but we stopped them easily enough. But once they got rather dangerous on a flank and the Berks, Bucks and Dorsets who had been in Reserve to our Division galloped up in the best of style, under a deuce of a shell fire and put things straight again, it was a splendid sight – that was when poor Phil Wroughton was killed.

We are now back having a real rest and I hope to go to Cairo in a day or so for six days' leave.

PS Perhaps I have said more than I should have done about the battle so don't make a song about it."

Chapter 6

An impasse was reached after the second battle for Gaza and for the rest of the summer the two sides faced each other along a twenty to thirty mile front. The Turkish forces occupied a line from Gaza, on the coast, to Beersheba, inland to the south east; the Allied troops on a parallel line from the Wadi Ghazze to Gamli. It was considered by both sides that any major campaign was impossible during the fierce heat of summer. It was also necessary for the engineers to continue laying the water pipe-line, rail and track, sufficiently far forward before any further advance could be considered by the high command of the Egyptian Expeditionary Force.

Anxious for a victory in Palestine as counter to the slaughter on the Western Front, Prime Minister, Lloyd George arranged that Sir Archibald Murray should be replaced as Commander-in-Chief by Sir Edmund Allenby, a soldier of imagination and initiative who had led the Third Army at Arras. The enemy also decided on some reorganisation. Erich von Falkenhayn, Chief of the German General Staff until 1916 and now commanding the crack Turkish and German divisions at Aleppo – known collectively as the Yilderim – moved south with his entire force, to organise the defence of Gaza.

Apart from occasional alarms and excursions and special operations such as the foray to cut the Turkish railway (letter 23.5.1917 refers) the Gloucester Hussars spent the summer fairly peacefully. Courses were taken and leave given; and for six glorious weeks the Regiment experienced a period of comparative rest at Tel-el-Marakeb on the shores of the Mediterranean.

Lt Wilson spent the first two weeks of June on another course in Cairo, this time on the use of the Hotchkiss gun and, in mid August, was given 7 days leave in Alexandria.

After Allenby's changes the regiment, although still with the 5th Mounted Brigade, found itself incorporated into the Australian Mounted Division. When Lt Wilson rejoined them in late August they had moved back to El Arish, now 40 miles from the front line.

El Fukhari   17.5.1917

"...the climate is totally different here to Sinai, or the grass and trees make it seem so. Every morning at dawn a fearful crowd of natives come by here, from the village on the way to the harvest. Some on camels, some on donkeys and some walking, but all kicking up the most infernal shindy. They come back at night with the camels carrying the corn – I took a few snaps and will send them as soon as they are finished.

(May 20th)

– Had to leave this letter for 2 or 3 days as we have been enjoying another dust storm which made writing impossible, but I'm glad to say it is easing down a bit now ..."

El Fukhari   21.5.1917

"...we had eight tanks with us at Gaza – I simply roared at them, it seemed too ridiculous for words to think they could wander about over the trenches and redoubts and we watching them one thousand yards off and afraid to peep at them except with one eye – sometimes we couldn't see them for shells, as a matter of fact, two of them got busted up – a direct hit from a shell plays old Harry with them – and they were lucky enough to put two in. I got to know one of the officers and had a look over his bus, they are most interesting, but the heat when they are in action must be simply awful.

Cavalry warfare is about over I think, as our infantry and the Turks are both pretty well dug in. They can't say we haven't done our share, we have taken every inch of ground this side of Kantara which is just about one hundred and fifty miles and I should think I have ridden on an average the whole distance at least three times – the Infantry have simply followed us up."

El Fukhari   **26.5.1917**

"... we have just returned from a very interesting two day show. We rode out to a Turkish railway just beyond Beer-Sheba, arrived there at dawn and blew about fourteen miles of it all to blazes besides three small bridges. Whether we took them by surprise or whether they were afraid of us I don't know but we met with practically no opposition and got back safely the next night with hardly a casualty in the two Divisions."

(Fara East Camp)   **6.7.1917**

"... we leave camp here for a month by the sea tomorrow DV from where we all hope to have leave. Our new Brigadier, General Fitzgerald, looked up the past work of our Brigade and he said we had done more work and had less leave than any Cavalry Brigade in the British Army ... so he is raising a fuss with the 'powers that be' and thinks we shall get a fortnight's leave each.

I collared 4 Turks the other morning but it didn't require much bravery as they were ready to give it up and two of them had discarded their rifles. The other two probably would have put up a fight only we 'came on 'em a bit sudden like' amidst a cloud of dust, and although they had their rifles loaded and cocked the worst they could do was to bring off a splendid salute. I borrowed a belt from one of them which has rather a good brass buckle with the Star and Crescent on.

We had a bit of a reconnaissance towards Beersheba yesterday but, although we got within 3 miles of it, we couldn't see it..."

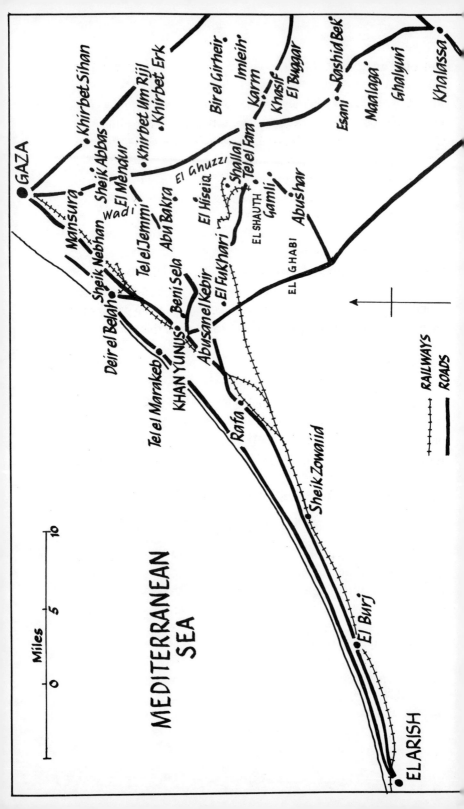

Tel-el-Marakeb   12.7.1917

"...I'm afraid I haven't written for nearly a week but four of us Lieutenants were sent to take part in the Review for our new Commander-in-Chief, General Allenby just arrived from France. It meant a lot of 'spit and polish' etc. and consequently no spare time – in the meantime the Regiment had moved back to the sea – where we are at present having a real rest: we sleep, eat, drink and bathe.

The inspection went off very well – we sat on our horses for three hours without moving an eyelash with drawn swords which ultimately weighed about five tons – whilst he rode round. This was after three hours of forming up and getting into shape – a battle is a picnic compared to a show of this sort."

Tel-el-Marakeb   24.7.1917

"... The natives have been having a rare time this month with their feast (Ramadan), they don't eat and drink whilst the sun is up but make up for it well at night. The last night of the month they feed the dead which is very amusing. We were riding through a village at midnight and as we passed the cemetery there was a most awful shindy going on inside. Every grave had a lamp burning on it, with a huge dish of meat and vegetables by the side. Hundreds of people were dancing and singing and the rest trying to keep out the hundreds of hungry dogs – who ultimately filled the role of the dead – from the grub. Soon after midnight the Mayor hunts all the villagers and as many dogs as possible out of the cemetery and the departed spirits may then feed. Wilkins was on guard over some walls nearby and he said as soon as the people had gone, dogs of all calibre rushed in and cleared up all the dishes – and so the poor dead had none. At dawn all the village turned out again and were quite satisfied that their lost ones had had sufficient food for the year."

Tel-el-Marakeb

1.8.1917

"… we are still at the same camp and having a good long rest. Our sports were a great success and everyone enjoyed themselves. We had a "Ladies" race the only qualifications being (1) to be as unladylike as possible and (2) to wear homemade ladies' togs. No one experienced much difficulty complying with the first, but the second was beyond the powers of any Hussar. It was very amusing, the General judged the Ladies and I took some snaps – I will send them along when they are finished …

August 3rd … I expect to take a bunch of men up to a Rest Camp at Port Said shortly for 8 days, which would be a nice change. We are stopping at this camp till the 18th – which will make a record rest of about 6 weeks – and then we are going to the front line for a while as we are joining a new Division. We are very lucky in dodging the hottest weather; by the beginning of September it will be quite cool again.

Fruit is in full swing here. Yesterday we were riding home and passed an Arab farm. For the equivalent of about 2/- [the farmer] let us go into his grape garden and fill our tummies up with the most delicious blue grapes and then we filled 2 or 3 nosh bags and brought them back.

You needn't think we don't live well – this was the MENU of our squadron mess two nights ago.

1) Soup
2) Rabbit (frozen Australian and jolly good), Taters and onions
3) Tinned fruit, Blancmange
4) Sardines on toast
5) Dessert: grapes, green figs, pears, melon
6) Drink: whisky, beer, gin, limejuice, ginger beer and tea.

A parcel arrived the other day in excellent condition after a 7 week trip and thank you very much. The pound cakes are by far the best thing you can send as that is about the only thing we can't get; but please .don't trouble about sweets in the hot weather as they get rather soft..."

Alexandria   **14.8.1917**

"... there is nothing much to do in Alex – and it is far too hot to attempt anything more energetic than sit on the beach and listen to the band – it is much hotter than Palestine. The journey here was pretty rough – I started from Rail-head at 5.30pm in an open cattle truck and got to Kantara on the Canal at 6.30am. I slept like a log from 8pm 'till 6.15. You have to lie down or else you would get tipped out – and there was a time when I used to get a headache if I went from Shrivenham to Swindon. At Kantara I changed on to the Egyptian Railway at 12.50 and got here at 9pm last night.

We had a huge horse Show the other day open to the Division (nine Regiments) and RGH did exceptionally well and took two-thirds of the prizes – my troop got two and if it hadn't been for bad management we should have got four. I entered my horse in the Heavyweight Chargers and, as he had been lame, I filled him up with corn to make him fat and didn't give him much exercise. He went round the ring with me and looked an easy winner, but the judge thought he would like to try him and just gave him a touch with his spurs – and then there took place a solo buck jumping display. We only just got the old judge off in time to prevent a catastrophe. The other bloomer took place in the pack-pony class (horses that carry machine guns). Mine was by far the best pony in the ring – but we couldn't leave well alone and tied about ten yards of ribbon round his tail which came untied and tickled his legs, which, combined with the joy of finding he had only got an empty saddle on him, was sufficient excuse for him to rush round the ring four or five times at sixty miles an hour. It caused great amusement though – the red, white and blue ribbon flying out behind made him look like a bird of paradise."

El Arish   23.8.1917

"... I have just returned from Alexandria after 7 days leave which I enjoyed very much and did me a lot of good ... I found the Regiment had moved back nearly 40 miles from the line, where peace reigns supreme; we can't even hear a cannon and very rarely see an aeroplane. We are living in a date and fig orchard; the former are not quite ready but the latter are just right. They make a welcome addition to our already excellent rations.

... I don't know what John Bull finds wrong with this campaign, he can't expect us to stride along without a check of some sort, we have gone nearly one hundred and sixty miles of the worst country in the world, driving the Turks out of at least ten or twelve strong positions, the Transport, Supply, Medical and Sanitary arrangements are absolutely perfect, everybody is merry and bright, and with ordinary luck we shall soon be in Gaza."

On 1st September 1917, I was naturally thinking about the opening of the partridge season at home. We were resting by the sea at El Arish, and had rolled the beach to make a cricket pitch that we surrounded with one strand of barbed wire. I was first to go down to the sea for a bathe the next morning and noticed something hanging on the barbed wire. To my surprise I found it was a quail and on looking around, I found another one. I took them up to the cook-house and asked the cook to serve them up on a piece of toast but not to bring them up until the Colonel, who I would arrange to be sitting next to, came in for breakfast. After the cook had pushed a dish of sticky porridge in front of the Colonel, he came to me and said, "And what can I get you, Sir?" "I think I should like a couple of quail on toast." He accepted my order and soon, produced them. The Colonel was very puzzled but I was not giving the game away. I was earlier still the next morning and, to my joy, I found four quail. So up to the cook-house again, and this time I told the cook he could ask the Colonel what he would like for breakfast. He came to me first and I repeated my order of the day before. Then he asked the Colonel who said, "Are there any more of those damned quail about?" The secret could be kept no longer.

After breakfast hordes of Arabs arrived over the desert and proceeded to erect miles and miles of nets and the following morning there were literally thousands of quail being collected. This was their migration and it lasted about a fortnight. One squadron had two quail per man for tea every day and the Sergeants' and Officers' Messes had them all day long. The only problem was getting them plucked and ready for cooking.

El Arish   2.9.1917
(to brother Jack)

"... I wonder if you had any birds yesterday.   We had quite a good day; seventeen mice during the night and we tried to catch a brace of sparrows during the day but they were too wild. I joined four Arab boys in an unsuccessful quail hunt this morning – the plan is to find a quail in amongst some brushwood (similar to the Rough common), place a net on the far side of a bush on the ground about forty yards in front of the quail. The rest of the hunt then crawl forward very slowly driving the bird – which is loth to fly into the bush that is netted, then rush forward as he flies out the other side (QED).

We are very short of officers just now and consequently I find myself OC Squadron "pro temps" which is rather good fun, and the higher the command the less you do."

El Arish

"... we don't think about the war once a month .. Teddy Townsend is a regular clown – he and I carry out military operations most nights. I'm General, he's OC flying machines and two or three more Second Lieutenants hold equally high appointments. Townsend usually goes bombing after dinner, he climbs up the Marquee pole about fifteen feet high and bombs the enemy with overripe figs. The only effective anti-aircraft guns are a barrage of glasses of beer put on the ground. When he thinks there are enough to bring him down he lets go and falls flat on the floor, but never hurts himself – he's just like a cat. You've seen photos of our bivouac tents, well, he *dives* over them and lands flat the other side time after time – and on hard ground too.

I hope the weather has [picked] up by now and that the harvest is finished – it is beautifully cool here."

Behind enemy lines. Film taken from a captured Turkish camera—and later finished off during Allenby's triumphal march into Jerusalem.

Wilson (*far left*) leading prisoners into Jerusalem.

A British tank put out of action at Gaza.

"War-baby."

Wilson with brother Teddy *(on left)*.

Wilson waters his squadron horses in the Jordan Valley.

The "Ambush Party" (led by Bob Wilson) at Hill 72. He later received the
MC for this piece of action.

After the charge at Huj, 8th November 1918.
(top) British horses lying close to the Austrian guns indicate that these Austrians continued to fire until they were galloped over.
(btm) Bob Wilson's shadow is apparent as he takes this photograph at Huj.

Chapter 7

October 31st was the date set for the renewed attack against Gaza but, for the Gloucester Hussars and Fifth Mounted Brigade the lull in the campaign ended with a move forward to Gamli – a point midway between Gaza and Beersheba – on 3rd October 1917. From Gamli front line patrols had several encounters with the enemy. On one of these occasions (16th October) Lieutenant Wilson's troop ambushed a Turkish cavalry patrol and he was awarded the Military Cross for this action. The Fifth Mounted Brigade was in reserve when the general advance began on 31st October. Allenby's 20th Corps of Infantry took Beersheba on schedule while the 21st Corps stormed the Gaza defences. The entire Desert Mounted Corps swept round to the north of Beersheba and spearheaded the pursuit along the coastal plain – taking Huj with what is considered to be the last cavalry charge engaged in by the British Army.

Hampered by lack of suitable tracks, insufficient water and supplies, and in the face of fierce enemy resistance, the Allied soldiers advanced fifty miles in ten days and took an estimated ten thousand prisoners*. The Gloucester Hussars were involved in the heaviest fighting and Lieutenant Wilson and his troop from D Squadron were again in the limelight receiving special mention for their part in the fighting around Balin, a station on the existing railway which ran from Beersheba to Nazareth. On 21st November D Squadron was seconded to Desert Corps headquarters – currently located at the small Jewish settlement of Rishon-le-Ziyon – and did not rejoin the regiment until late December, after Allenby's triumphal entry into Jerusalem on 11th December.

They spent Christmas, as did most of the mounted troops, clearing the area north east of Jerusalem in filthy conditions, attempting to repair roads and damaged wells.

---

* Estimates vary, but 'ten thousand' is the figure quoted by Field-Marshal
  Viscount Wavell, Allenby, Soldier and Statesman, George G Harrap & Co
  Ltd, London 1946

MEDITERRANEAN
SEA

Tul Keran

NABL

Arsuf
Kalkili
Jijulie
Mesha
El Lubban

JAFFA
Sarona
Selmeh

Ludd
Budrus
Midieh
Shilta
Suffa

Ramleh

Kubeibeh

YEBNA
Deiran

JUNCTION STATION

Saris

JERUSAL

Bethlehe

Esdud
Termus
Balin
Sumeil

El Mejdel
Julie

Solomons
Pools

El Faluje

Arak el Menshire

Beit Hanum
Nejed
Tel el Hesi

Hebron

Umbrella Hill
GAZA
Tel el Negileh

Hareira
Sharia

Tel
el Jemmi
Shellal

Karm
Bir es Sakaty

BEERSHEBA

Khasim Zanna

Esani

Khalassa

Asluj

MILES

5   0   5   10

+++++ RAILWAYS
ROADS

El Auja

"... we haven't done any fighting but frequently have big reconnaissances out Beersheba way, one of which was what the Turks called a victory and you mentioned in your last letter. They always claim to have driven us back but we simply go back just to go to bed. I was in charge of a little ambush a few nights ago, and played Merry Andrew with a few of their cavalry and pinched some lances and brass stirrups – irons and bits, besides a lot of other stuff which I had to hand in to HQ. Teddy Townsend is still all right but very worried. He is trying to discharge the duties of Intelligence Officer and we [often] pull his leg. If we are on patrol or anything he comes to us at once for any informaton and we tell him any rubbish we can think of and when he has made it all out nicely we quietly hand him in a report. Its as dark as pitch and I have no candle so must ring off."

When on a small patrol one morning I was fortunate enough to capture a Turkish cavalry officer. What attracted my attention to him were his stirrups or irons, as they are called. His spurs and the horse's bit were all made of shining brass and I had never seen this, before or since, so I decided to take possession of them. The other thing that took my fancy was a beautiful pair of Zeiss field glasses hanging around his neck, and I relieved him of that burden as well. When I took him up to the Colonel and handed over his revolver and one or two papers, the Colonel asked, "Is that all he had on him?" I don't think I heard and, in any case did not answer and took the first opportunity to slip away. The Regimental saddler made me a beautiful case for the glasses and, at the very first point-to-point I attended after the war, some "crook" pinched them out of the case."

…You will be very surprised to hear that I have been 'awarded the Military Cross' – it came through two or three days ago, I will enclose the Telegram – I expect it is something to do with the ambush business I told you about in another letter – the Sergeant and Corporal I had with me both got the Military Medal."

Beersheba   6.11.1917

"…Just a few lines to let you know that I am quite well and very happy despite the recent battlings which to say the least has been rather strenuous. You will see by the address that we have taken Beersheba, it was a great show, we galloped it from behind whilst the Infantry came at the front. We took their guns, eight hundred horses and no end of prisoners and we have now paved the way for our comrades to do the same with Gaza and I'm thankful to say they won't be able to use us there … poor old Wilkins got hit in the leg but is not very bad."

I don't remember being desperately hungry, but on occasions we had to suffer agonies of thirst, and then the very strictest discipline had to be enforced. I have seen an officer jump up in the firing line and start running towards the Turks, who were desperately defending some wells about two hundred yards away, when we had been without water for nearly two days in the hottest of weather. We managed to stop him, but he said "If they have got water, I am going to ask them for some." He was, of course, temporarily demented and had to be sent to a casualty clearing station.

We had eaten nothing all day and just as the sun began to disappear I remembered I had a very small tin of runner beans in my haversack – not so large as a small teacup. When I had eaten them there was about a teaspoonful of liquid left in the tin and, although I was tempted to drink it, I thought that perhaps someone might be in greater need, so I poked it under an over-hanging rock to keep it as cool as possible. The Turks and Germans, with their stomachs full of life-giving water, launched a violent counter-attack in which we suffered many casualties but managed to hang on. It was now quite dark and the shooting fizzled out. I saw someone being carried down the terrible rocky hill by four men. It was Lieutenant 'Wilkie' Wilkins, he had been seriously wounded and was only just conscious; I trickled the spoonful of bean water into his mouth. Although he never rejoined the Regiment he came to stay with me several times after the war and always said it was the best drink he ever had. As an indication of the state of exhaustion we had reached I think twenty-two men had to be called on – in turn – before he was safely carried to the bottom of the hill – probably no more than sixty yards.

I had intended avoiding as many details of actual battles as possible especially in cases that were accompanied by the loss of good friends, but I feel justified in telling what I know of the brilliant cavalry charge at Huj on 8th November 1917. Firstly because I did not share in the glory, and secondly because there has been quite a spate of correspondence in the papers recently,[*] endeavouring to establish the last real cavalry charge to be made by British troops.

If what I saw on 8th November 1917 was not a cavalry charge there has never been one. My Brigade, the 5th Mounted, were pursuing the retreating enemy but, owing to the difficulty of watering the horses, we could never catch up with them. What water there was in the area was chiefly in deep wells and, after the Turk had helped himself, he smashed what lifting gear there was and did his utmost to ruin the wells. As a result he could travel as fast on his flat feet during one night as we could in twenty-four hours on horseback. I have, on more than one occasion, queued up with my Squadron from dark to dawn

* 1971

waiting our turn to water, and then had to resume the march next day without having had any.

On this day, the 8th November, the Brigade was being led by two Squadrons of the Worcester Yeomanry and one of the Warwicks, with the Gloucester Hussars in reserve. For some time we had realised that the enemy was at last making a stand, as considerable artillery fire was coming our way. We were advancing in line, well fanned out – on very tired horses – when I detected a gradual quickening of the pace but could get no orders from anyone, as the Colonel and Adjutant were out of sight most of the time, hidden by folds in the ground. Eventually we found ourselves doing a good gallop and, as we crossed the ridge there was revealed a scene witnessed by few men – enemy heavy guns and machine guns surrounded by their crews dead or wounded as were many gallant yeomen and the horses that had carried them as hunters over their farms at home. I am not particularly emotional but this was the most distressing thing I had ever seen.

The first man I saw was a friend of mine in the Worcester Yeomanry whose horse had been killed under him and who had been killed by a bayonet obviously before he had a chance to put up a fight. The next sad sight was of a sergeant in the Warwicks who I also knew; his horse dead on its knees, wedged between the wheel and barrel of a heavy gun. The sergeant was dead in the saddle and the Austrian gunner was dead with the sergeant's sword through his chest and his own rifle still in his hands. The only section of the enemy force to stand their ground were the gunners, mostly Austrians; the guns were manned and fired to the last second by these green uniformed fellows. The Turkish infantry was still scuttling away, occasionally turning to fire a few rounds but our horses were still without water so any further pursuit was out of the question. We buried those splended yeomen at dawn and, for the first time, realised the wicked waste of war. I will not presume to give the names of these light-hearted heroes; in the hunting fields of three counties some of their names were household words. Colonel Gray-Cheape of the Warwickshire Yeomanry led the charge, as one would expect of one of the world's best polo players and, although, he came through safely, he was later to lose his life when the ship on which he was travelling to France was sunk by a torpedo. There were seventy-five casualties from three squadrons – a heavy price to pay.

I pulled up by my Colonel, Lieutenant Colonel A J Palmer, DSO and, as soon as we had got our breath, he told me to find a doctor and do what we could for the wounded. I was fortunate in spotting a very sulky looking German officer with an armlet denoting that he was a medical officer. He was smoking a cigarette and appeared quite uninterested in the wounded. He spoke perfect English and I told him to get on with his job. To give him what little credit he was entitled to, I must say that he appeared very skilful and impartial. He had dressed the wounds of about ten or twelve men and was kneeling at the side of the next one when he looked up and glared at another casualty lying about twenty yards away. This was a poor old Turk with only a few minutes to live and someone had covered him with a coat. My doctor 'friend' sprang to his feet and raced across to him. I ran after him but was not in time to prevent him from snatching the coat and throwing it away, at the same time giving the groaning Turk two or three violent kicks in the ribs. When I started to give him some of his own medicine he justified his action by shouting "Look – a Turk covered by a German cloak!" The Turk was lying close to one of the guns and had undoubted-ly received this small act of mercy from a gentlemanly Austrian. Incidentally it was a most elegant garment, beautifully cut with a very posh waist and plenty of skirt – a typical cavalry cloak. The weather had started to turn cold and, as our winter kit was many days march behind us, I wore that cloak for two or three days until the Colonel said "I should take that off if I were you Bob, somebody might shoot you." Somehow I managed to hang onto it and brought it home with me nearly eighteen months later.

Nr Hebron **12.11.1917**

"… We have been very busy lately since we took Beersheba on the first. We have chased Johnny Turk till he has been hunted out of his positions one after the other and has retired to a line practically at Jerusalem. I am writing this under a railway bridge about twenty miles from there; we have given up the chase owing to there being no live Turks within reasonable distance and because our horses are beat to the world – some of them have had no water for more than three days.

The day before yesterday our Brigade made a charge with the sword that should become famous. We went straight at three batteries of guns and a machine-gun redoubt and polished off the whole outfit. We collared twelve guns besides the machine guns, they fired their guns till the Warwicks were within ten yards. Am glad to say our casualties amongst men were very few – but a lot of horses were killed – the Warwicks and Worcesters got the worst of it – fortunately the RGH were the third line. It has been a complete rout, the country is strewn with all sorts of things from guns down to cigarettes."

(cont'd) **13.11.1917**

"… we were called away in a hurry last night so will carry on now. Some Turks were reported at a station about seven miles up the line, three Brigades of us galloped up there in pitch darkness just in time to find the whole place and stores etc, in flames but the Turks managed to get away.

Although transport has been very difficult we have done quite well with regards to food – a lot of fowls, goats, sheep and tame pigeons having fallen into the stock pot. The Turks draw their heavy guns with oxen which are not very dainty, but better than nothing. We killed one at Beersheba – a regular old stager – we cut him up and carried him about and cooked him whenever we had half an hour to spare and in a few days he got quite tender."

Rishon-le-Ziyon   22.11.1917

"... Have been too busy to write anything till now, but at last we are more or less settled down. Our Squadron is now doing escort to Corps Head Quarters which is an ideal job – we are at present living in a modern Jewish village built by Rothschild, the people are all fruit farmers and we buy practically anything we want. We have a roof over our heads which is a great advantage as the winter is in full sway and we get very heavy rains. We have done a lot of fighting since my last letters and all has gone well – we have not actually taken Jerusalem but last night we had driven them out of all their trenches and the town itself was under rifle fire so we expect any minute to hear that it has fallen. I was within eight miles of it the other night, we went past Bethlehem, but not actually in the village, but hope to have a look round when things become more normal. The Turks have made two very strong counter attacks with German Divisions and our Brigade met both of them which was rather unfortunate as each time the odds were 10–1, but we stopped them till the infantry came up.

We are expecting to keep this job till after operations, so DV shall have a good time – we can't even hear the guns."

I met Lord Allenby twice; the first time he said "Good Morning" and the second time, "Good Health". I had been sent with my troop as his escort on some ceremonial parade. This was at a little Jewish colony called Rishon-le-Ziyon where I had recently been attached to General Head Quarters with my troop, and become friendly with the local doctor and the Mayor who was a considerable maker of wine. After the parade my troop and I made it convenient to call on him, and we each came away with two buckets of very new wine. It is quite easy to carry two heavy buckets on a horse by putting your toes first in the handle of the bucket and then into the stirrup, and you would hardly know it was there. We were, of course, taking it back for the Regiment but after we had gone a little way we pulled up for a rest and to have a taste of the wine. We were sitting in a circle on the sand, passing one bucket around, while the other twenty-five buckets were together a few yards away. Suddenly – out of the blue – the Commander-in-Chief, complete with his staff and pennant flying, nearly galloped over us, and kicked volumes of sand into our precious wine. We did not have time to get to our feet, let alone stand to attention. He just waved, shouted, "Sorry" and then, "Good Health."

Rishon-le-Ziyon   24.11.1917

"... we are still living in the Jewish colony and doing escort at Head Quarters. This is quite an up-to-date place; although it has no name it possesses a barber, two cafes where we can get a passable tea, a butcher shop, school, synagogue and a huge wine distillery where they make wine from the grapes grown in the village.

This civilisation comes as a great relief to us as it is the first we have struck in the two hundred miles between here and Egypt which has taken us nineteen months to cover. I went to an orange grove yesterday and bought forty huge Jaffa oranges for 1/- besides picking as many as I could eat. We have taken Jaffa but so far I have not been there. Head Quarters will no doubt move there shortly; they say the town is in middle of hundreds of acres of orange trees – it is a lovely sight to see them growing.

About a week ago we had two days rest by some water

where a few ducks came to feed at night – it was the most dangerous part of the war I have been in yet. Crowds of fellows were waiting for them, Yeoman, Highlanders, Indians and wild Australians armed with revolvers, rifles and even machine guns and whenever a bird of any type appeared there was a terrific fusilage as if the whole Turkish army were advancing. Our casualties were slight – one Australian having his leg broken – and we killed about seven ducks and eight coots which usually becomes the property of a non-combatant who was hero enough to dive into a storm of bullets and bring the bird back into our lines."

4.12.1917

"… the nuts you sent were excellent – they travelled well, but am sorry to say the apples could not stand the strain. You see, they are handled about such a lot *en route* viz: by post to Southampton, boat to Boulogne, then boat to Alex, motor lorry to HQ (sorted) … train to Kantara, ferry over the Canal, military railway to Gaza – from there fifteen miles per camel and then pack horse to within ten miles of Jerusalem the Golden."

10.12.1917

"…Jerusalem surrendered last night…we are still doing escort and by the time we finish the rest of the Brigade will be back refitting etc; they are at present in the front line but we hear from them that everything is very quiet. The rains have now started in earnest – simply poured all day yesterday and all night but we managed to get a room in a house close by. The inhabitants are very hospitable here, we spend a lot of evenings with the local doctor, a Russian; his wife and sister-in-law speak English very well. He is coming to tea with us today – I don't know what he will think of our manners and army rations.

All the people are Jews and profess to be very pious, they

nearly faint if you try to buy anything from them on their sabbath, but they don't mind looking the other way whilst you help yourself to what you want and they don't forget to turn round in plenty of time to see you put the money on the table! About the only place you can buy 'bacca is in the synagogue."

Rishon-le-Ziyon   16.12.1917

"... we shall DV remain here until after Xmas and we are gradually getting our Mess stores up to strength, sufficient to stand a strong attack on that day.

You have, of course, heard all about Jerusalem. Very satisfactory to have taken it without [knocking] the Holy Places about. I went to Jaffa a day ago and had a look around, it was very interesting indeed. Some of the buildings down by the Docks looked millions of years old, some of the streets aren't wide enough for two people to ride abreast. There is, of course, a modern part of the town consisting of everything up to date – larger shops, a Bank (German) and Town Gardens with a band-stand – but most of the wealthy people cleared out, being Germans or Turks.

I sent a small parcel of things the other day; its 10–1 they don't reach you but in case they do they are: 1) 5 glass knife rests I took out of the Turkish Officers' Mess after the charge, (2) a very ungainly looking necklace which the Arab women wear. Inside the cylinder thing they carry a few words of the "Koran" (a sort of Mohamaddin (sic) Bible which they use when they want to "offer up a short 'un"). Inside that I put 2 prs cuff links, a snuff box, bracelet and a thimble which I got at Jaffa as souvenirs... The flower is Mimosa, I picked it on the road to Jerusalem during the scrapping – about 12 miles from there – the nearest I have been so far ... "

While 'D' Squadron did escort duty at Desert HQ the rest of the

Regiment fought its way inland to the north-east, bypassing Jerusalem itself. They were involved in heavy fighting at El Burg facing a strong counter attack by the enemy and also had to contend with the unusually heavy rains and cold of early December. On 9th December Jerusalem surrendered without a shot being fired; the Turks having already evacuated the city.

It was Christmas Day and we had been sent up to the mountains to help the Infantry who were in some sort of trouble. We had left our horses and transport in the plain at the foot of the hills with the minimum of men to look after them, when the most violent storm broke out. What had been dry transport and horse lines were, in less than an hour, under water and from where we were we could see the men making valiant efforts to save horses and wagons. Their efforts were not sufficient and we saw two or three wagons and mules washed out to sea. It got colder and wetter every hour and we had no shelter, except for a ground sheet, which was not very adequate on a rocky mountain with a continual cascade of water running down. On my brief spell off-duty I arranged some branches of olive trees which just kept me above water with something like a mill-stream running beneath me. We managed to collect a certain amount of drink for Christmas and we were all so cold, wet and miserable that ‒ despite the proximity of Johnny Turk – who we assumed must be as miserable as we were – we cut down a number of olive trees, soon had a roaring fire going and started our Christmas celebrations. I managed to sidetrack a bottle of gin and went in search of Bill Rickards, second cousin of mine also with the Regiment, in pitch darkness, and eventully there was a response to my shouts of "Corporal Rickards." I found him trying to get some sleep on tree branches with his ground sheet tightly stretched over him. I pushed the bottle under the sheet and he told me next day that he sucked it dry straight away.

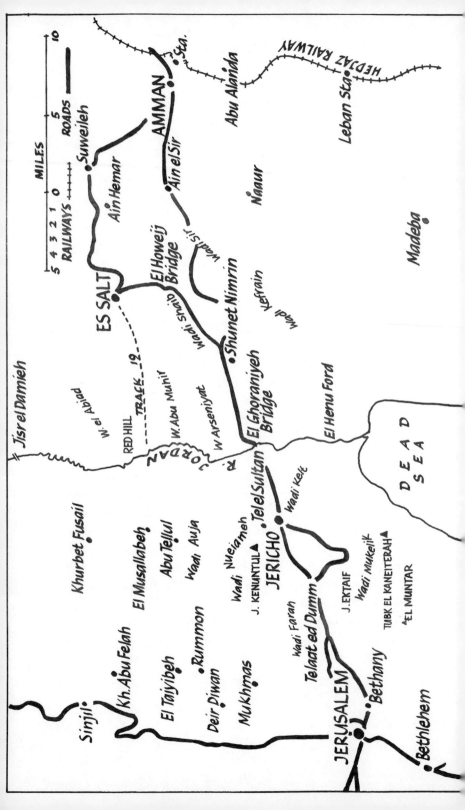

Chapter 8

The line north of Jerusalem remained static until April. Allenby's plans for a further advance were postponed as demands from the Western Front in Europe took priority. Many of the experienced troops, including Yeomanry regiments, who had been serving with the Egyptian Expeditionary Force were sent to Europe and replaced by Indian and Anzac units. The Royal Gloucester Hussars joined with the 18th Bengal Lancers and the 9th Hodson's Horse to become the 13th Cavalry Brigade.

The most important event for Lt Wilson at this time was that whilst in Cairo on a cavalry course in January 1918 he met his future wife Edith Ross (known as 'Paddie'), a young VAD then working at the 70th General Hospital, Abbassia. He then rejoined the Regiment at Deir-el-Belah, south of Gaza, where intensive training continued – along with home leave for some, courses for others, trips to Jerusalem and the Divisional Sports for all – until the end of March.

On April 1st the Royal Gloucester Hussars started to move to the front and by the 5th had arrived at Selmeh, a few miles to the east of Jaffa, where they set up camp. On the 24th they moved off again, traversed the Judean Hills and came to rest 3 miles north of Jericho on the west bank of the Jordan. On the 29th of the month they crossed the Jordan at Ghoraniyeh Bridge to participate in the second attempt to take Es Salt, the first, in March, having failed. Es Salt was a forward defensive position for Amman, a town in a commanding position on the Hejaz railway. Allenby launched this attack ostensibly to cut the Turkish supply line and aid the Arab Northern army which was approaching from the south but also to divert attention from the area of his intended coastal offensive. Es Salt was taken but could not be held and, amidst heavy fighting the regiment re-crossed the Jordan on May 4th.

Early in June Lt Wilson went off to another course in Cairo, this time on topographical reconnaissance, followed by a short leave in Alexandria with Paddie now at the 17th General Hospital, Alexandria. This meeting was not without its problems but, by September, they were officially engaged to be married. Lt Wilson rejoined the regiment about 7th July for a second, much shorter, spell in the Jordan Valley which they finally left on 3rd August going first to Solomon's Pools then, via Jerusalem, to Sarona on the coast to the north of Jaffa, in preparation for the next, and final, active phase, the "Big Push."

Deir-el-Belah   **9.1.1918**

"… tomorrow I go to Cairo for *nine days leave* and without asking for it – it gave me the surprise of my life when I was asked if I would take it – and after that I do a three weeks course, so I can reckon on nearly five weeks civilisation.

I rode through Gaza yesterday, I never saw such a mess in my life, practically every house is knocked down and I don't think it can ever be replaced.

A year ago today we had the show at Rafa and are having a celebration dinner tonight DV. We have a very comfortable Mess, dug out in the sand with a tarpaulin roof and two good tables and forms which have found their way here during the darkness of night. Some poor General will probably eat his dinner off his lap tonight; we live by robbing our friends."

By far the most important thing that happened to me in Egypt took place at the pyramids, when I met my wife "Paddie" Ross, who was a VAD.

Three of us were on leave and having tea at Mena House, which was overlooked by the Sphinx, when the local tram arrived from Cairo. Three VADs got off, had tea at Mena

House, then walked up to the pyramids. We followed and, while they were at a fence admiring the view, joined them and offered them a lift back to Cairo in our taxi. One of them had to be back on early evening duty so we tossed up to see who would take the other two to dinner at Shepherds Hotel. The toss decided that I was one of the two escorts. For the last sixty years whenever I wished to be particularly rude I would say, in front of my wife, that to this day I cannot decide whether I won or lost the toss!

I probably asked her to marry me that day; anyway I pestered her to such an extent that when I was up at the front several months later, I received a telegram to say that she would take me on. Paddie kept in touch with the other two VADs, she did not see much of "Bunty" Baker-Jones but Josephine Davis "Davey" was a close friend until the latter's death. "Davey" was one of the first VADs to go to France early in 1915 and was there during the battles for Loos and the Somme where she earned the Mons Star and was mentioned in despatches. After recovering from an illness she was sent to Egypt where she stayed until she was demobbed in 1919.

Cavalry School Zeitoun   28.1.1918

"...Cairo is beautiful in the winter, the best climate you could strike I should think. I went to Church yesterday morning and enjoyed the Service very much, and two or three of us went out to the Pyramids in the evening. Townsend is down here too, so we keep each other company..."

Deir-el-Belah   25.2.1918

"...I got back to the Regiment yesterday and found them still in the same place and doing anything but soldiering – football-,jumping, racing – hunting takes place every day and the big race meeting is fixed for 9th March.

I met a topping little VAD whilst I was there (Cairo) she used to go to church with me and sometimes lunch or dinner. There was nothing much in it, but you get so fed up with soldiers' company that its a nice change – she is an Irishman."

Deir-el-Belah   27.2.1918
(to Paddie)

"... I probably shan't have much time for writing next week, as we have to go up to Gaza to pull down old Turkish works etc.

I'm feeling very "stuck up" just now as I have become 2nd in Command of a Squadron. I'm not altogether pleased as it means parting with my troop – the best lot of fellows this world ever saw. Its rather strange but after a bit of scrapping and roughing it, discipline vanishes and a troop becomes more like a big family – that's why I hate leaving them.

The weather is rather devilish up here compared to Cairo – a regular hurricane comes along every night and usually flattens our tents and bivouacs unless we hang onto them like grim death. I pity the poor girls who are coming up to this hospital..."

Deir-el-Belah   15.3.1918

"... HRH the "Dook"* and Mr Allenby came up yesterday, inspected our Division and gave us our medals. General Hodson got a CB   he commands the Division; General Kelly our Brigadier got a CMG and DSO; Colonel Palmer a DSO; and Captain Mitchell and myself MCs. All the rest got an orange and bun – we all handed the medals back again and they are returned to London where they will be engraved."

Selmeh   9.4.1918

"... We have now become settled down at a camp just
* The Duke of Connaught

outside Jaffa – living in acres and acres of orange trees in full bloom and the blossom smells A1 ...

On our trek here we camped at Ashdod where the Ark rested I think and another night we camped by the mouth of a Wadi (river) where Jonah was too tough for the whale.

Perhaps you have heard rumours of troops being sent away from here but we are stopping – for the duration I think – and possibly 50 years after that..

PS Talking about Samson – one of our officers had a chap in his troop called Simpson and he told him to move a huge log of wood, but the fellow said, "Pardon me, Sir, my name is Simpson – not Samson."

Selmeh   **17.4.1918**
(to Paddie)

"... We have just come in from rather a sentimental parade – the Brigade turned out to bid farewell to the Worcesters. It was fairly sad as we had fought side by side from the very beginning and had made some jolly good pals.

The flies are a devil of a nuisance, simply swarms of them and such active creatures too. I wonder if you could pinch about 2 square inches of muslin or something that I could utilise as a fly net ... Teddy Townsend tied a fly paper up in his shack yesterday when there was a very rough wind blowing and caught practically everything but a fly – handkerchiefs, socks, ties, etc. etc."

En route to Telaat-el-Dumm   **25.4.1918**

"... I am writing this during a halt – we are trekking across the Hills of Judea – the scenery is beyond description, some of the valleys are almost perpendicular and you can hardly see the bottom of them. The hills are literally covered with hundreds of wild flowers of all colours and shapes. We shall see the Holy City tomorrow and Jericho the next day and if we are lucky we may get a wash in the Jordan in about four days' time – anyway we don't look like getting one before."

The summer of 1918 proved our greatest ordeal. It was decided that the Jordan Valley had to be occupied to make possible the autumn campaign that was being planned.

It was generally accepted that no white man had ever before lived through a summer there and even the flies died of the heat. The Turks cheered us up by dropping leaflets telling us that, "Flies die in July, men in August and we will come and bury you in September." The only sign of life, apart from every type of reptile and insect, existed at the little monastery – a building that looked as though it had been stuck on to the perpendicular, rocky wall of the valley and to which "naughty" monks were banished as punishment. If the idea was to cool them down a bit it was something of a sick joke; if it was to prepare them for the afterlife they had not much to fear from eternity.

Our unpleasant companions included scorpions black and yellow, huge tarantula spiders and, even more venomous, centipedes six inches long with pincers that could inflict an almost fatal injury. Once, in the middle of the night, there were cries of agony from my troop sergeant who had been bitten by one. He was in terrible pain, his arm visibly swelling. The doctor did what he could but the sergeant had to be evacuated to hospital in the morning. Deadly snakes, including the "horned viper" which actually killed two or three of the Australians, were there too. I had spread my blanket one evening before turning in, and went to have a last look at the horses. When I cam back someone shouted at me not to lie down as a snake had just gone under the blanket. We gathered round – armed with various weapons. I had a very swish riding cane with a brass ferrule on the end. As soon as the blanket was snatched away I saw the snake coiled up in a compact little circle, no larger than the top of a tumbler. I immediately gave it a terrific whack with my cane, right in the centre of the coil and, when I lifted the cane, he was hanging onto the brass ferrule. He went over my head like a whip; they were as quick as that.

One of our troopers had a fighting scorpion that lived in a cigarette tin. It was the reigning champion, the victor of about a dozen contests. Someone else had a fighting tarantula with an equally illustrious record, and a fight was arranged between them. As soon as they found themselves in the ring – usually a cardboard box – they sensed what was expected of them but, on this occasion, both looked surprised to find themselves opposed to members of a different race. After a bit of preliminary sparring which went in favour of the scorpion – naturally more nimble on his feet than the spider – who obviously felt he had got his opponent weighed up. He sailed in to deliver his blow, which took the form of a rapid swing of his long tail over his back and head. But the spider also knew what to do. He just stood his ground then, with one nip, pinched the scorpion's tail in half and leisurely proceeded to devour his foe. It was a sad trooper who threw his cigarette tin away.

When we were being relieved, or being sent down to relieve another regiment, it was a very tricky operation. The roads and tracks were so narrow for the first five or six miles out of the valley that one regiment could not pass another. As these changeovers had to take place during the hours of darkness it meant that the valley was, in fact, completely unoccupied for several hours – so the movement had to be carried out very quietly and unobtrusively. There was a sort of lay-by at a spot called Telaat-el-Dumm which consisted of a solitary stone-built ruin known as the "Good Samaritan Inn." There was just sufficient flat space for one regiment to park while the other went by. It was not unusual, when waking the men to resume the trek, to find one or two dead. The sudden change in altitude added to the exhausted condition we were all in after a month in the "Valley of Death", was too much for those with the slightest weakness of constitution.

The fact that there was plenty of water in the tributaries of the Jordan eased our misery considerably. Food was not much of a problem as nothing was appetising and, as soon as daylight arrived, everything was smothered with flies and hornets – monstrous things about twice the size of a wasp and equipped with a terrible sting. I once, unknowingly, led my troop over a hornet's nest at a walk and was surprised to see one trooper's horse gallop past me like a racehorse. He had let go of the reins and was covering his face with both hands. Then I noticed he was covered in hornets and a whole swarm of them were clustered around the top of the horse's tail. We were at a standing camp at the time which was fortunate, as the horse had its head in a water trough and the trooper, still in the saddle, was practically unconscious. His face was so swollen that he was unable to see for days and he spent a long time in hospital. A day or two later the horse started to lose its hair and soon became completely bald.

Wadi Auja   **7.5.1918**
(to Paddie)

"... The stunt is not quite over but we are more or less stationary for a day and I hope to get a chance of posting this – it is the first opportunity I've had of writing to you. The first week we spent behind the Turkish line which naturally interfered slightly with the postal arrangements.

We were about 15 miles east of the Jordan and the country was really topping – all sorts of birds and flowers and the cuckoo used to hollow [sic] at us every morning which reminded us all of the old country ... We are now on the banks of the Jordan, its a rotten sort of place and the mosquitoes are big enough to carry bombs. We are still very busy and rather tired, we didn't average 2 hours sleep for the first 9 nights..."

(to Paddie)   **11.5.1918**

"... this will be a short note as we are literally tormented with flies and consequently I want to shove my head into that fly net you sent me... this cursed Jordan valley is the most astounding place imaginable: dust about 6ins deep, flies and mosquitoes by the million and a continuous hot wind blowing which makes you think you are looking into an oven... Must ring off now as I'm going out with the Artillery Officer to try and get his guns on to some Turks that we can see out in front ..."

Jordan Valley   **18.5.1918**

"... we are in the same district but in a far nicer camp – within ten yards of a lovely fresh water stream, and as you may imagine we make the best of it. We spend our spare time either washing or drinking tea – milk, tea and sugar are quite plentiful enough for us to have tea six times a day, hitherto water had been the only difficulty.

I am expecting to go to Cairo on 3rd June for another course of a month – it will take me about three days to get down. I shall ride to Jerusalem and get on the Turkish Railway and go from there to Ludd (Lydda in the Bible) and then "Right Away" I can do with a change again and I shall just escape the hottest month of the year DV.

Thanks very much indeed for the parcel of sweets, biscuits and the mince-pies which were perfection. The night they arrived Cripps (the Brewers at Cirencester and a Lieutenant with us now) and I had a long patrol to do along the banks of the Jordan; it was a roughish ride through Jungle two or three yards above our heads and took us pretty well all night. I had put the mince-pies in my haversack and, much to Cripps' astonishment produced them about midnight.

Must ring off now as it is getting late and we rise at 3 o'clock every morning, in good time for milking."

I had one good meal in the Jordan Valley. I had offered to do the midnight patrol for another subaltern who was 'under the weather' and there had been a rabbit issue. This item on our menu will always remain a mystery to me. Their journey commenced in Australia and brought them to Kantara half way down the Suez Canal where they would be transferred to the railway and, after a few days, might reach Railhead There they would probably be delayed for three or four more days while being allotted to different units. Then they would be placed on to camels – or later on, when we had reached some roads, on to lorries – and would eventually arrive at our own cook-house. When they were unpacked there would be a layer of ice between the skin and the flesh. The British troops liked these rabbits; they were really excellent and much larger than our English rabbit. The Australians, of course, would not touch them, and called them "bloody rats".

On this particular patrol one never got back until 2.30am but Coombs, my wonderful batman, said he would have something ready for me. On my return I found a small table and chair and the table laid for a one-man banquet with a candle burning in a jam-jar. Coombs soon appeared from the cookhouse with a whole rabbit, beautifully roasted, with stuffing and potatoes and a billy-can of strong tea. What the stuffing consisted of I shall never know, I was afraid to ask; but sitting there alone under a full moon, with the camp asleep all round me, and peaceful pipe of tobacco after my meal, is still one of my most happy recollections of the war.

Cairo   4.6.1918

"You will see that we have once again reached civilisation –
Cornwall and I are down here for a month. It is quite cool after
the Jordan Valley and we are making the most of our chances of
enjoying the change.

The journey was a bit teasing, we were in some trenches
when we left – which was on Wednesday – we reached our
horses that night, found our kit and slept there. [We] started off
to Jericho at 6 in the morning, picked up a motor lorry there
about midday, got to the Holy City at 4 o'clock and stopped
there the night in goodish quarters (Fasl Hotel). I found a new
pair of underpants in the bathroom, an item which I was in need
of, so I appropriated them.

We had a look around the Holy City in the morning and were
both very disappointed, you want to be full of imagination to
believe half of it. Calvary, the Garden of Gethsemane and the
Golden Gate are the only genuine things and of course, they do
bring a lump in your throat. The Holy Sepulchre was the most
disgraceful display I have ever seen, one mass of gaudyness –
dozens of flags with rubbishy designs on them, paper flowers of
every colour and the whole thing apparently designed to make it
as little sacred and impressive as possible. To put the finishing
touch to it they have dotted horrible trashy wax-works of Christ
and the Virgin Mary at various places. I felt quite wild to think
that a place which could be made to mean more to a Christian
than any other should be so hopelessly spoilt by the money-
grabbing Greeks, Armenians and any other sect that could
creep in.

That is how they do it, each sect grabs as much as possible of
the Holy spots in order to get money from the tourists. Even

the manger in Bethlehem which only measures about 8 feet, is divided between 3 religions and then they quarrel and fight. Only the other week a man was killed actually on the spot because he wanted to pinch an extra inch or two ..."

Helouan, Nr Cairo   25.6.1918

"...our course lasts another week and then Palestine again. We are all enjoying it very much, the last week we have spent at Helouan, a health resort just outside Cairo – we are living in the best hotel in the place and are becoming quite gentlemanly again. We came here because the country is supposed to be suitable for reconnaisance training but I think the real reason is that the instructor is a first class sportsman and thinks we deserve a spell of civilisation.

I met an Australian Sister last night who married a friend of Major W Frogley's in Salonica. She knows him very well and says he is known as "Poodle-faker" or "afternoon-tea king" and that he has a friend in every hospital. The VAD is in Alexandria now, and so I probably shan't see her again – and what is more I shan't lose any sleep over it either... We have concerts in the Hotel every evening which are quite good.

There are lots of Italians, Greeks and French people here and two of the Italians are Opera singers – a lady and a "bloke". Some of their duets are really top-hole but fade away before our united efforts with *Polly-Wolly Doodle* and *Clementina*. We always have to render these twice or sometimes three times to satisfy them – they simply howl with laughter although they cannot understand a word.

My humble rank naturally precluded any contact with the Generals – higher rank than Brigade or Divisional Commanders – but, on the three or four occasions that I did meet them I have reason to remember little incidents. The first one I must not name. He was a very nasty gentleman who was carrying out an inspection of the Regiment when I had the misfortune to be temporarily in command of the Squadron. I met him as soon as he arrived at the head of the Squadron and gave him a very proper salute, which he acknowledged with a very rude stare and no word of greeting. I fell in about a stride behind him and, in the first troop, we encountered a Corporal wih a very accentuated 'door mat' moustache. The General glared at him for some time then turned to me and shouted "Is that Charlie Chaplin?" I had already sized the man up and, although everyone else had heard him, I pretended that I had not. "I beg your pardon, Sir?" at which he pointed at the – by now – rather embarrassed Corporal and said, "Is this Charlie Chaplin off the cinema?" I replied, "No Sir, that is Corporal Simpkins" as bluntly as I could to let him see that I was not impressed by his type of humour. "Then tell him to save the bloody thing off."

The next troop offered no opportunity for his sarcasm but the third one made up for it. There was a period when junior officers, especially those in the Cavalry, had the habit of producing very elaborate salutes. The hand would go up so energetically that it would quiver for a few seconds in front of the face, as if the enthusiasm engendered by a meeting a General coud not be restrained. This particular Troop Leader's efforts easily outshone anything that even I had seen before and I knew, at once, that I was in for more trouble as this form of salute was not popular even with the senior officers of our own Regiment. The General just said, "Good God" turned to me, looking as if he had just seen a ghost, and continued, "Did you see that?" I felt increasingly rebellious. "No Sir, what was it?" By now I was really asking for it – "That salute, or whatever it was." I still pretended I had not seen anything unusual so he yelled in my face, "Tell him to do it again." I very quietly said, "Green, the General wishes you to salute him again," although I made a point of not saying "properly". The next effort was no better. The poor General turned away in disgust and his remarks were quite unprintable. "Make sure he has a fortnight's saluting drill."

The fourth troop passed muster and I might have disposed of the little man at this stage but for the fact that, as was sometimes the case, he asked to see the "sick lines." I had no sick horses but put two of the worst looking ones on a line by themselves – just to humour him. To show that he had not finished his 'cat and mouse' game, he growled, "Any sick horses?" I said there were two and he said he wanted to see them. An officer had always to be responsible for the sick lines and I had given the job to a very newly joined youngster for the simple reason that I thought he would be out of harm's way. The cavalcade walked in silence for quite a distance for this final scrutiny. The General pointed his stick at one of the horses, "What's the matter with that one?" Young Gaydon, playing for safety answered, quite truthfully, "We are not quite sure yet, Sir." "Not sure! Haven't you diagnosed it?" "Oh yes, Sir, three times a day." Even the General was reduced to a "tut, tut" by that and walked hurriedly away.

The average temperature taken on the hills at the side of the Jordan Valley was 113 degrees in the shade, with a maximum of 122 degrees. At the Ghoraniyeh Bridge* over the Jordan, the most vital point to safeguard, it reached 130 degrees in the shade on several occasions and once touched 132 degrees. The poor horses suffered terribly and we had to keep three or four blankets over their backs all day long to prevent heat stroke to their spines. Added to this discomfort, we were forbidden to take them to water during daylight as they would stir up 'dust devils' hundreds of feet high which immediately attracted heavy firing from the hills on the eastern side of the valley.

In the evenings we revived quite miraculously and felt fit for anything. The Turks and Germans also appeared to appreciate change from the usual boredom and each night patrols would

* See map

116

clash and some little half-hearted sort of scrap would break out. One night it became obvious that something more ambitious was on their minds. We were 'standing to' long before dawn when there was a very short, but heavy, artillery bombardment which lasted for only two minutes. When we had recovered from this rude disturbance and, as it got light, two or three silent batteries of German artillery became clearly visible. It gradually dawned on us that they were ripe for the taking – which we did without any unpleasantness. While this was going on several hundred unarmed Turks – grinning from ear to ear – started dribbling in and giving themselves up. The reason or this rather easy victory lay in the fact that relations between Turk and German were not too happy. Owing to the difficult terrain over which the German artillery had to travel only the very minimum of ammunition could be carried, and this had been expended in the first sudden disturbance. The role of the Turks was to carry the 18lb shells on their shoulders, but after humping this burden for two nights, they became "browned off", called it a day and failed to do their duty at the vital moment. They then realised they were between the devil and the deep blue sea and preferred surrendering to the risk of retaliation by the Huns.

This haul of prisoners was the largest of the campaign to date and it was decided to make a propaganda film of masses of German and Turkish prisoners being marched through the Holy City. I was ordered to make myself as smart as possible and pick twenty of the best turned-out men in the Regiment to provide the escort. The prisoners were very cooperative and I had no difficulty in getting them marshalled just outside the city wall. When the camera arrived, on a very shaky lorry, and had taken aim, I was told to move off but to halt when the end of the column had passed the camera. The lorry would then go on ahead, take up a position opposite some other historic point, and the camera would start grinding away again. After this had been repeated two or three times I was very flattered when the man in charge of the filming asked me if I would be good enough to change my position in the column occasionally, as I was too conspicuous, and unfriendly people would recognise the whole thing as a fake. It wasn't my personal beauty but that of the very lovely jet black horse I was riding – one of the twelve, I think, that mobilised with the Regiment with Corporal Bridgeman, and remained there until the Armistice. Although this horse was my most precious possession for nearly three years there were many occasions on which I should have been delighted to shoot him. I must have ridden him thousands of miles and, of course, he was always sweating. Every few yards a bead of sweat would settle on his belly; he would think it was a fly, put in a false step, and try to swat it with a hind foot. This, coupled with the fact that I nearly always had a splitting headache during the heat of the day, made me feel like murdering him.

Khurbet Beit Sawn   16.7.1918

"… we shift camp again tomorrow – it will take us about twenty-four hours – we leave here at 2.30 tomorrow and arrive in Jerusalem in time for dinner which we have ordered in advance. We then push off again and arrive at the Good Samaritan's Inn about 6am where we can get some water, leave there the next evening and arrive at our destination about 2am.

They brought a lot of Germans over here – apparently to have a go at Jerusalem – they attacked two or three days ago and got a very nasty smack in the face. I had the pleasure of escorting about six hundred of them through the Holy City last night. It was quite good fun and the population went mad with excitement. We went through a regular barrage of cinema cameras.

I have been OC Squadron for a few days – whilst the Squadron Leader is on leave – and as luck would have it, the Divisional General came to inspect us. He is a very grumpy old man and shouts out the most impossible questions. I managed to answer them all pretty well until he said in a very mild sort of way "And how are you this morning?" I was too overcome to speak, just bowed my head and looked dumb – he went away satisfied that he had me beat."

Jordan Valley   1.8.1918

"... we are going back by Solomon's Pools – which are huge reservoirs by the side of the Hebron—Jerusalem road, about ten miles from Jerusalem, built by Solomon to supply the Holy City but, like the one that Pontius Pilate built about seven miles further down the road, it was of no use as Jerusalem stood a few feet higher than the pools and they couldn't get it there. But we have fixed up some tremendous engines to supply the whole place from the same pools; this has been done to gain favour with the people more than anything else and is excellent propaganda. Before, the only water they had was what they stored in cisterns during the winter."

Jerusalem   21.8.1918

"I am writing this in Jerusalem – we are on our way to the coast, thank goodness. The Regt. passed this way last night but I'm going over by train tomorrow with all our kit, stores, etc. Palestine can't be a very huge country as a couple of night marches takes us from the Dead Sea to the Mediterranean, but, my word, there are some differences in the climate.

...I am not afraid of France, as a matter of fact I should like to go there, but I won't if I can help it for your sake – and I don't think we ever shall. Already there is a minimum of white cavalry here and we are mixed up with Indians, really good soldiers who fight like tigers.

Major Turner has returned ... he had an amusing time coming

through Italy, he was fetched off the train and sent on a "joy mission" to celebrate the Italian victory. He went over the country being feted and receiving bouquets from little girls, imbibing champagne and standing to attention whilst bands played *God save the King,* and leading huge processions and all the time saying nothing but "Viva l'Italia" – which he afterwards discovered is grammatically wrong. He had a liaison officer with him to make all the speeches whilst the Major smiled and bowed. He makes us roar when he tells us all about it, which is very often!"

Chapter 9

The Royal Gloucester Hussars were in the forefront of the "Final Push" through Palestine and into the Lebanon which began dramatically on 19th September 1918. Cavalry units raced fifty miles up the coast in twelve hours and were conspicuously in the lead for the first twenty-four hours. Allenby's meticulously devised campaign of deception had worked brilliantly: the enemy had prepared to face a thrust north from Jerusalem.

It must be said that, at this stage, Turkish resistance was already crumbling; their forces on this front were outnumbered and inadequately supplied, the men undernourished and decimated by sickness. Turkey's ally Bulgaria, had already collapsed and Germany was facing defeat on the Western Front. Some of the Turkish troops and the men of the Yilderim offered stout resistance but the majority fled northward.

The "other jaw" of General Allenby's planned pincer – the Arab Army of the North – had played its alloted role by harassing and immobilising Turkish forces east of the Jordan and by isolating the remaining enemy garrison at Medina. This Arab Army welded together with considerable diplomacy by the Emir Feisal – son of King Hussein of the Hejaz – was a polyglot of some twenty thousand regulars, frequently Arab and Turkish deserters, and an estimated ten times that number Bedouin irregulars.

Since November 1917 Allenby's "Hejaz Operations Staff" had co-ordinated, supplied, financed and supplemented this loosely-structured fighting force. T E Lawrence, Dawnay, Joyce, Newcombe, Peaks and other attached British officers and men with the aid of Indian units of the Camel Corps, French machine-gunners and a "Flight of Aeroplanes" had achieved the seemingly impossible. Both jaws were set to close on Damascus as envisaged by Allenby.

The latter, instinctively, held back his own mounted divisions and gave the city to the jubilant Arab Army of liberation.

The Desert Mounted Corps were then given the task of carrying on the pursuit to' Aleppo. Like many of the soldiers in this campaign they were now severely affected by malaria, the worldwide epidemic of Spanish Influenza and general debilitation. Lieutenant Wilson was with the Regiment until it reached Baalbek where he collapsed, a victim of malaria.

It is now a matter of history that Lord Allenby's preparations for his final breakthrough were successful beyond all expectations.

It was necessary to concentrate his main forces and, at the same time, convince the enemy that the attack would come from the Jordan Valley. Troops would leave the Valley during the night, their camps left standing, with two or three men remaining in each camp to light fires and kick up as much dust as possible. Dummy horses were made of blankets and poles to give the impression that they had arrived during the night. Every day a force of Infantry marched down the Jerusalem–Jericho road and were brought back by lorries during the night. This task was left to the British West Indies Regiment who enjoyed the gentle stroll downhill and the motor ride back in the evening.

Our Brigade, the 13th Mounted, consisted of the Royal Gloucester Hussars and two regiments of Indian Cavalry and we were given the honour of leading the "breakthrough." We had spent three of the most pleasant days of the entire campaign living in the orange groves at Sarona near Jaffa so that we should not be seen by enemy aircraft. The shade of the trees and the delicious fruit, added to the anticipation of a really gallop, put us on our toes. By midnight, 18th September the whole of the 5th Cavalry Division had moved down to the beach

Miles
0   5   10
ROADS
RAILWAYS

MEDITERRANEAN SEA

L. Hule
Jisr Benat Yanuk
Safed•
Capernaum•
SEA OF GALILEE
Mejdel•
Tiberias•

ACRE
Sherif Amr
HAIFA
Kefr Kenna
El Meshed•
Bridge
Jeida•
NAZARETH
Jebata
Mejeidil•
Junjar•
Abu Shusheh
Jarak•
Afule
Shulton•
Sindiane
El Lejjun
Zerin
•Dufeis
Beisan•
Ez Zerg Heniyeh
Liktera•
Jenin
Jelameh•
•Mukhalia
Tul Keram
Samaria•
NABLUS
Balata•
Tabsor•   Kalkili•
Bir Adas•   •Jiljulieh
erekiyeh •Kefr Kasim
Sarona
FA
El Lubban
Eurkha
APPROXIMATE ENEMY LINE
SEPT 19 1918
R. JORDAN

and, although closely formed up, we must have stretched for three miles along the sands. The excitement seemed to extend to the horses, they had been well-watered and fed and, as we lay on the beach in front of them, there was a continuous, contended champing of bits. We had been so well briefed and drilled that no one doubted the successful outcome of the operation, and we were told our objective was Damascus.

It had been hoped that the infantry and artillery would have made a gap in the enemy lines by 10am when we should go through and cut off any survivors. However, so severe was the barrage of over four hundred guns on one small sector which burst like thunder on an unsuspecting enemy at 4.30am that we received the order to mount and gallop on at 5.50am. This was a real thrill for all of us and I, of course, had the father and mother of all headaches. Coombs, my devoted and invaluable batman, had just fitted my tourniquet with two nice smooth pebbles from the beach in time for me to move off at the head of the Division. I had previously been ordered to provide the right flank guard and to get as far ahead as I could. We were told not to bother about any prisoners but to keep moving on. We overtook hundreds of bewildered Turks and Germans still plodding along in the same direction in which we were heading. We just waved to them and pointed in the direction from which we had come. Some took the tip and started going back, some just sat down and lit a cigarette and some even prepared meals – but none offered any resistance.

All the while there was a huge column of enemy guns, wagons, cavalry and stragglers moving north, parallel to us but about a mile away. I was not concerned with them as I knew they were destined to be cut off by the 4th Cavalry Division which was operating on our right. I had reached a convenient little hill that just provided cover for the horses and decided to let them have ten minutes rest. By sitting on top of this little hill I could, by using my glasses, observe all the enemy movements on my flank and also follow the advance of our Brigade. Below this vantage point were three Arab shepherds sitting and watching the huge enemy column. They were, no doubt, puzzled at the sudden activity, probably thinking of some rich pickings later on and quite unaware that my troop was within fifteen yards of them.

Suddenly, one of the Turkish cavalry detached himself from the column and came hell for leather straight for my little hill. I crawled down just below the crest and said to Sergeant Stock – my most excellent troop sergeant – "Two of you get mounted and, when I put my finger up, you can gallop round and collar a very dashing Turkish officer." He galloped straight up to the shepherds and was yelling at the top of his voice, obviously asking for information. He was a very smart gentleman with an impressive row of medal ribbons and he was mounted on the most beautiful Arab pony. When I raised my finger Sergeant Stock and a corporal dashed round the hillock, one each side, seized a rein each before he could move, and led him round to me. I gave him a friendly salute and a reassuring smile as I patted the pony's neck. He was still being held by both reins when he suddenly dug his spurs into the pony and away he went – nearly knocking me down. He had to do a sort of semi-circle to get clear of the troop and he produced his revolver and had six shots at me whilst he was doing it. We were all quite unprepared for this and rifle bolts started clicking but I shouted at the top of my voice "For God's sake, don't fire." Neither the brave little Turk nor the superb pony deserved to be hurt. I watched him safely rejoin his regiment and chuckled to myself when I thought of the story he would relate. I did not mention this incident to my CO.

The Brigade pulled up for a short rest after eighteen miles of this thrilling run and found water for the horses and a meal, of sorts, for the men. At 6pm we moved on again for Nazareth – another forty miles – which had to be occupied before daylight.

This time the 18th Bengal Lancers were leading, and there has never been a worse forty miles of riding by night. Confusion was complete; the way was over sheer rocky mountain and we kept losing sight of the man in front. Several times we had to remove the packs from the machine-gun pack ponies to squeeze them through cracks in the rock and when the packs had been replaced, we would be in a dark desolate world without a clue as to the direction taken by those ahead. By some miracle we eventually found ourselves on the reasonable going in front of Nazareth and gradually became united again. Either the 18th Bengal Lancers were not where they should have been – or we were in the wrong place ourselves – because the Lancers were supposed to have blown up the railway about one and a half miles south of our crossing point. Instead, just as my poor old horse was gingerly feeling his way over the track, there was an almightly explosion about ten yards away and a piece of railway track, about two yards long, buzzed over my head.

This disturbance, plus a sizeable battle taking place at the railway junction El Afule, a few miles south of us, should have given the enemy in Nazareth some warning of our presence. As it was essential that we should be in occupation before dawn we hurried on and, at 4.25am precisely, we saw Nazareth, drew swords and charged down the streets. Some of us had previously been given instructions to capture General Liman von Sanders, the German Commander-in-Chief. The idea was to take two tough troopers and a horseholder, try to locate his HQ, and fight it out with his guards before they had got the sleep out of their eyes. There was, of course, great rivalry amongst us for such a prize. Whilst my little gang was busy shedding anything that was not required for the immediate job, a small four-wheeled carriage came flying out of a side street. The driver, a civilian, was standing up and flogging his poor horse with a whip as hard as he could. Out of the corner of my eye, and in the half light, I saw that the occupant was a rather important looking officer. I was on my flat feet, but a very new and keen young officer, Lieutenant Petty, was close to me and still mounted. I yelled to him, "Catch him, Petty, it could be his Lordship." Petty was off like the wind and, when he drew alongside the carriage, he poked his revolver – and almost his head – through the window. The gentleman inside accepted the challenge and a duel took place at full gallop. Pop, bang, pop, bang in turn and just when I thought there had been two 'maiden overs', the Turk got Petty 'LBW' with his last round, hitting him in the knee. It had been amusing to watch, but, unfortunately, the wound turned out to be quite serious.

My party – Corporal Hambling, Trooper Hargreaves and, of course, Jack Taylor to hold the horses – galloped right into the centre of town and found a good spot, at the back of a big building, for Jack and the horses. The town was gradually waking up by now and a terrified old man peeped out of a doorway. With all the ferociousness I could muster I shouted 'Commandant.' He brightened up at once, obviously willing to help, and pointed to a large well-built edifice.

I did not think it looked a likely place for the Commander-in-Chief to choose, but I still think the old man thought he was doing the right thing. It was about a hundred yards down the street and we raced off as fast as we could. My fears were immediately confirmed; we had arrived at the barracks and about one hundred and fifty unarmed Turks casually walked out on the parade ground and formed themselves into quite a respectable parade, with only the least encouragement from me! I was bitterly disappointed as it was obvious that I had gone to the wrong place.

After a few minutes the prisoners started talking in small groups and this developed into giggling and laughing. One of them stepped out of the ranks, came up to me, pointed to a long row of windows on an upper story and hurried back to the ranks again. I thought this upper story should be explored and as

Corporal Hambling was quite capable of looking after the mob we had already collected, Hargreaves and I went into the building. I left him at the foot of the stairs and went up until I found myself in a long corridor with about twenty rooms each side. I was, by now, equipped with a revolver in each hand, a week's growth of beard and still wearing Coomb's tourniquet; I must have looked more like a pirate than anything else. I hurled myself at the first door and was confronted by a smiling, bowing officer who immediately proffered his revolver and sword. I thanked him very much and told him to go downstairs where Hargreaves was waiting. After hurling myself at two or three more doors and being received in the same gracious manner I simply opened the door and walked into the remaining rooms, with an occasional trip to the top of the stairs to ask Hargreaves if the prisoners were behaving themselves. In each room the occupant went through the same procedure, handing over revolver and sword and, sometimes, maps and papers, and I soon had several heaps of weapons along the corridor.

Eventually I came to the last door which was very firmly bolted and barred. I thought of doing the 'Western' stunt of shooting the lock off but didn't know how to do it. It all seemed ominous as I could hear movement and whispering going on inside and I thought that I had at last reached the hornet's nest. I flung all my weight at the door which crashed open. I was prepared for anything – except the tableau which confronted me. On the floor on his knees, with hands clasped in prayer, was an officer and, on the bed with no blankets or anything, a woman and her baby – born only a few seconds earlier – which had yet to offer its first squeak. This had me beaten, of course, so I just shook hands with the officer, patted the woman on the head and pinned a notice on the door warning all troops to leave them in peace. I am glad to say that they had the opportunity to get away safely as, after a few hours of comedy, we were pushed out of town and did not recapture it until the following day.

When I got downstairs again I found a perfectly orderly parade awaiting me but an uproar, like a football crowd, coming from another part of the barracks. I went to investigate and witnessed a horrific scene. In a huge dark cavern of a place guarded by a massive iron gate were probably a hundred of the most filthy objects that ever existed. They were obviously prisoners but whether civil or military it was impossible to tell. There was literally nothing in the way of sanitation and the floor was nearly six inches deep in the most putrid and evil-smelling filth. As far as I could see in the near darkness there was not a stick of furniture and they must have been sleeping in this muck for months. Their clothes were in such a state that it was hard to tell if they were wearing khaki or navy blue. They looked and behaved like animals rather than human beings, screaming and pulling away at the iron bars – some on the shoulders of others. I decided that they had earned full remission but could find no other exit and the barred gate would have defied a Samson. Then I realised that they were pointing across to a small block of offices and begging me to 'apply within'. I went across and walked in and there was the most immaculate gentleman sitting at a desk, with a self-satisfied grin on hs face and a huge bunch of keys hanging on his belt. He was obviously the gaoler, and I made it quite clear to him that I wanted the place unlocked but he was very reluctant to move. I was in a hurry and he very nearly lost his life. I expect he realised that possibility and lazily rose from the chair and strolled across to the gate, unlocked it and made a dash for safety. The poor wretches flew out through the gate, danced and shouted with joy, and to my disgust, even tried to embrace me. They were followed by a swarm of flies that literally darkened the sky.

The released prisoners very willingly joined the parade and I called Hambling and Hargreaves over to have a look at the conditions in which the poor devils had been living. I had quite forgotten the gaoler until I saw him quietly strolling back to his office still swinging his bunch of keys. I invited him to join the party but he was most indignant and refused and once again he nearly lost his life. When, at last, we had prodded him along by the sharp point of a sword applied to his bright blue pants, he was greeted by jeers and threats from the rest of the gang.

By this time there was quite a battle going on and I realised that my hopes of going down in history as the man who caught the Commander-in-Chief were ruined. I had started the morning with enthusiasm and confidence and it now dawned on me that all I had achieved was to console a terrified father, comfort a pain-wracked and hysterical mother and give freedom to a most pathetic lot of prisoners. It had all been a waste of time because the genuine prisoners of war had – without exception – leant over backwards to give themselves up! It was some consolation to learn later that Liman von Sanders had not been at home anyway; ironically, about four nights later I had to pass through Nazareth with just my troop and I thought it would be a good idea to spend the night there. To my joy I discovered that the Town Mayor was a friend of mine. He was in the Connaught Rangers and, being a very efficient sort of soldier, he had been sent to take over the administration of the place whilst we pushed on towards Acre and Haifa. He was occupying Liman von Sanders' house and I spent the night in the Commander-in-Chief's bed, between silk sheets that were decorated with his enormous monogram. In the wardrobe was his full-dress uniform complete with medals and, in the cellar, dozens upon dozens of bottles of champagne. "Nobby" Clarke was a real friend that night as we had no rations of our own, and his batman provided an excellent dinner as well as providing for the troop, who also had their fill of champagne.

After sending Hambling and Hargreaves back with our assorted prisoners I went in search of Jack Taylor and our horses. What I had thought to be a nice safe place behind a large building was the one spot in the whole of Palestine that I should have avoided – as far as Jack was concerned. In the darkness I had failed to realise that it was the one and only respectable hotel in the place, obviously patronised by the German Staff Officers, and I had left Jack by the cellar door. I found the four horses all right, their heads all in a bunch filling the doorway, but there was no sign of Jack. Then I noticed that only mine had reins on; the wicked old rascal had removed the reins from the other three, joined them together end to end, and buckled them to my horse's bridle. With a few pieces of rope added he must have had a 'life-line' of about forty feet which I followed down a winding stone stairway until I found myself in a huge cellar. There was Jack sitting on the floor, drunk as an owl, surrounded by hundreds of cigars and a dozen or more empty – or partly empty – bottles of every description. He was entirely oblivious to the noisy battle going on at ground level and the fact that he was in some danger of being cut off. "So glad you've come" he said, "I've found some wonderful Scotch." I could not stay long but I made it my duty to explore the cellar whilst I had the opportunity and Scotch was the one thing I failed to find.

I took what samples I could carry, including some really superb sparkling Hock and a box or two of cigars, and bundled Jack up the stairs. I then saw that he had not been idle and had also thought of his comrades for a bottle was attached to every available buckle and strap. By the time we got the reins sorted out and Jack was on board again, Hambling arrived to tell me that my Troop was in action in a large Monastery garden. It was on the other side of town and only approachable across about two hundred yards of very open ground. This was no sort of track for Jack with four horses jingling all the way with his bottles so I decided to send him back to where the led horses of the Regiment were positioned, and slip across by myself to join the Troop. I got all four horses' heads facing up the street in the right direction and said to Jack "Now just go as if the devil was after you," gave the horses a good crack on the rump and away they went. I watched their progress for a moment and then, to my horror, the whole outfit crashed to the ground amidst clouds of dust. I concluded that he must have been caught by the stream of machine-gun fire but, as the dust cleared, I was relieved to see they were all on their feet. Jack did not try to remount but just ran for his life, the horses very obligingly jogging along with him. But where before had been bottles of priceless liquor, the straps and buckles were now carrying broken bottle necks.

I had sent Hambling back to tell the CO we were all right and that I was going to join my Troop. I did the trip across the open bit of ground without incident and found my Troop blazing away over the top of the very high Monastery wall. They were standing on trestles and tables with a number of wicked-looking old monks – who were enjoying themselves immensely – occasionally pointing out a target and giggling with glee if someone appeared to score a hit. They had also shown the Troop considerable hospitality and everyone was happy. I then got a signal that the Regiment was retiring and we were to join them at once. Monks and troops shook hands a dozen times as if we had been friends for years and then I realised that I was the only one present without a horse. I saw the troop safely away then poked my nose round a very wide doorway in one corner of the wall. I was greeted by a stream of machine-gun bullets. I tried the door in the other corner with the same result. The wall was far too high to climb so I made my way, in something of a quandry, to the Monastery to see if I could find a rope or something to haul myself up.

I did not relish meeting the monks again as everyone in the Holy Land had a habit of changing his allegiance to suit the existing situation. Fortunately, I was spared the risk as I stumbled on a ladder which just reached the top of the wall. That was miracle number one, and miracle number two followed immediately as I cautiously peeped over the wall. Standing just below me was a magnificent donkey, apparently asleep and in any case taking no notice of the noise, complete with saddle and bridle. I dropped right at his head (cowboy fashion) and was in the saddle in a second. This really roused him and we were off like lightning. The machine-guns opened up when we had gone about half way and we went even faster. By this time the Regiment could see what was happening and we were urged on by cheers and, I regret to say, laughter. The Colonel came up and said, "That's the best donkey I've ever seen – can I have him?" I was only too pleased to oblige and I think it is true that the donkey carried the Colonel's spare kit until the end of the war.

Hargreaves and I were allowed to go back into the town again to see if there was any sign of Von Sanders' HQ but could not get very far. We had to lie down in a very narrow pathway with tiny houses on each side, and could not see anything or anybody. About every two minutes a rifle would go off within a few feet of us and the only place that seemed capable of holding a sniper was a small out-house a few yards away. I made up my mind that immediately after the next shot I would rush in and see if that was the gentleman's hiding place. I sprang to my feet, put my revolver round the door and was on the point of pulling the trigger when there was a shrill female scream. There was the sweetest little Eastern lady complete with 'yashmak' – which could make the dullest woman look beautiful. After satisfying myself that she was the only occupant and carrying out a tactful and respectful search, I decided there was no danger from that quarter; although, strangely enough, there was no firing whilst this episode was taking place.

We lay down again still puzzled and then a hand-grenade came over the house on the other side of the lane and landed just in front of us. We covered our heads with our arms and awaited the explosion. It never came and when I peeped to see if it was still smoking, I could see that it was just a pomegranate which is exactly similar in appearance to a Turkish hand-grenade. Comedy again. Further down the lane was a rather more pretentious house with a small garden in front and to our surprise, the door opened and a woman said in perfect English, "Would you like a glass of water?" The effects of Jack Taylor's cellar were now sadly worn away and a glass of water was the one thing we needed, so we rather foolishly walked up to the door and stood – one at either side – whilst the lady was pouring out the water. Suddenly Hargreaves gave me a violent blow in the chest that sent me staggering backwards and, as I fell, I found myself looking straight down the muzzle of a rifle held by a Turk with a smile on his face, as much as to say "Got you at last". He was less than five yards away and fired – but where the bullet went I shall never know. The lady slammed the door and disappeared while Hargreaves went in hot pursuit of the Turk and ran him to ground, appropriately enough, behind an ornate tomb in a nearby cemetry.

Things quietened down after this but we noticed considerable activity at a large building down the street which we approached with great caution. There was no need for caution, however, as the scene now changed from comedy to sheer revelry. This was the hospital which was dispensing first aid and hospitality quite impartially to both sides. Captain Gilholm, a regular soldier attached to us, was sitting on a wooden chest with his arms round an attractive, giggling Armenian nurse who told me, in good English, that they intended to get married. Gilholm just said, "Hello Bob, come along in" as if he was running the show, which, in fact, he was. Everyone was so happy – Turk, German, Englishman all shaking hands and beaming – that I hated to have to tell Gilholm that he was somewhat isolated, as the battle had moved on and I thought we had also better be moving. So, after friendly farewells and a touching scene as Gilholm and the nurse kissed each other good-bye, we left. Some of the Turks were not wounded or sick but it never occurred to us to ask them to come along as prisoners.

By the time we rejoined the rest of the Regiment we found

that a withdrawal had been ordered to El Afule. Unfortunately the Australians had been there before us and, having a natural "nose" for gold, had swiped all they could carry of the beautiful golden sovereigns. The place was littered with paper money but we realised with the departure of the Turks this currency was now worthless. Teddy Townsend and I picked up a £25 note each: they were huge and most elaborate things to look at. I offered mine to a woman in Nazareth the next morning for two eggs, but she would not do a deal, fortunately for me, as I think it later saved my life in Beirut. Teddy brought his home and four or five years later got £7 for it at his bank.

We had intercepted a lorry full of drink and, amongst other items, I acquired a bottle of Cognac. I had been carrying on my sword hilt for weeks and weeks a Christmas pudding, still in the basin in which my mother had made it, awaiting a suitable occasion. This bottle of brandy seemed ideal for the job, so five or six of us sat round a fire, heated the pudding, soused it with brandy and set fire to it. We drank the rest of the bottle along with three bottles of excellent sparkling Hock – a very pleasant evening under the shadow of Mount Tahor.

We had to occupy Nazareth again in the morning which we did without any opposition. I looked for my lady and new-born baby but they had evidently managed to get away. We had to put out an outpost line during the night but did not anticipate any trouble as things had been quiet all day, and patrols had moved a considerable distance forward without any sign of Turk or German. Charlie Byard – our machine-gun officer and a natural clown – was taking care of the road leading north. His machine gunners were covering the road while Charlie was having forty winks in a small building nearby. My troop was on high ground to his right and there was some Indian Cavalry to his left. Suddenly, about midnight, out of a perfectly peaceful, silent night, there was a most terrific shindy on the road below – not much shooting but a lot of shouting and swearing. Three or four figures came running up the hill to me and were, fortunately, challenged when they might easily have been shot instead. They were Charlie Byard's machine gunners and very angry, "The bastards sprung up from behind some rocks and collared all our machine guns before we could move," which was probably correct as the disturbance lasted only about a minute and was followed by complete calm. I ran down to Byard and found him still having his forty winks. I had great difficulty explaining the situation to him, he kept saying, "I can assure you Bob, old boy, its nothing more than rumour." He had got one boot on and I was putting his revolver and tunic on him at the same time, when there was another fearful flare-up on the other side of the road. We saw the Indian Cavalry, the 18th Bengal Lancers – dismounted – making a wonderful bayonet charge on the skyline. Besides inflicting heavy casualties they came back with three hundred prisoners and Charlie's machine guns – still intact. Thus, our entire machine-gun strength had been lost and found again before Charlie got the other boot on.

We returned to our former positions and all was quiet until a sentry nudged me and said "Look, there's a bloke coming towards us." He didn't appear to be a very good scout and, instead of taking as much cover as possible, seemed to choose the highest boulders as his pathway. The sentry challenged this visitor who appeared to take no interest but came stumbling towards us. At last someone opened fire and eventually the target sank down among the rocks. At dawn we were very sorry to find that he was a large performing bear – still wearing his "chain of office."

The next morning – the whole 5th Cavalry Division – started at 4am to deal with Haifa and Acre. Haifa was thought to be the more strongly held and the 14th and 15th Brigades were detailed there whilst we were sent round to the north of Acre to cut off any escapees and hold the town. The war was held up for an hour or so when we were entertained by some very pretty dancing ladies at a small village where we had found some water for our horses. The dancers and musicians were really good, the instruments tuneful and the little episode served as a tonic. No doubt, while we were being entertained, someone from the village was running to Haifa and Acre to warn them. But the war had to go on and very shortly Haifa and Acre appeared in view, and it was obvious that the two Brigades attacking the former had not encountered any entertainment delay as we could hear them in action.

We soon came under some feeble artillery fire but gradually approached the town across a fertile plain. I was with the CO and, through our glasses, we observed a gentleman in a black suit riding a donkey, an umbrella in one hand and a white flag in the other. Major Turner very brightly said, "That looks as though they are chucking the sponge in. Gallop into the town and try to find some grub." I passed the gentleman on the donkey; he raised his hat with both hands as, being encumbered by an umbrella in one and a white flag in the other he was unable to let go of either. I galloped into the small square in the centre of the town where the local lads were looting the olive oil store, a huge underground affair and, as far as I could see, the only real asset in the place.

They ran past me without taking the slightest notice, every vessel full to the brim. Just as I got to the store one of them was pushed into the tank and I could see him blowing bubbles from at least three feet below the surface – which gives some idea of the amount of oil there was. Nothing short of shooting would have stopped the looting and, as I was alone and still had to hang on to my horse, I settled for two canvas buckets of oil for myself. Not that we had any need of it but I hoped to exchange it for an egg or two with some old lady unable to take part in the "free for all." This proved a good idea and I soon had to return for more oil. I was in the town for more than an hour leading my horse from door to door and acquired quite a sizeable stock of eggs, fruit – and even a chicken – to take back to the Major. No-one had shown the slightest resentment of my activities and some displayed such lack of respect that they never even glanced at me, and the oil boom was still going on when I left.

Acre   24.9.1918

"...This is my first letter since we started on the push. The RGH created a record I think – we broke the Turkish line about 7am on the morning 18th and by 4.30am the next day had galloped to Nazareth, capturing about 2,000 prisoners chiefly German*, and on the way we had a lot of scrapping and took about another 6 or 700 – which was 66 miles in 22½ hours and 2,600 prisoners. You never saw such fun in your life as we had at Nazareth, only our Regiment were in the town they didn't expect us at all and were all in bed in different houses. Those we woke up of course were easy prey but street fighting of the very first order soon developed and lasted nearly all day. Major Howard, myself and three men went to the Barracks and collared twenty-two officers and any amount of men – all the officers were in separate rooms but we put our shoulders against the doors and fell through and bundled them out very unceremoniously. We then rang up HQ on the phone but only being able to use Berkshire language coloured with a little Billingsgate we didn't learn much.

The town is quite a good size and full of English speaking people – the Germans did themselves well, and for the last week the humblest RGH trooper has smoked nothing less than a 9 inch cigar or drunk less than Hock – and often Champagne.

All the time we were scrapping from house to house, the Church bells were ringing and people going to Church as if nothing was happening. We have now pushed on and taken Haifa and Acre† – beautiful places with histories – and good bathing – and I think the fighting is about over now. Men and

* Official records put the figure at 1500 or 1600
† Acre was not actually taken until several days later

horses are in good fettle but naturally tired."

We stayed in this very pleasant seaside town all the next day. This was the thirteenth time the town had been taken in its long history and, in the little fort which was being used as a hospital, I saw many cannon balls still imbedded in the walls – some of Napoleon's perhaps. During the day I had been sent on a foraging mission. Most of the cattle and sheep, for which the district was well known, had apparently disappeared 'under the counter' but I succeeded in getting sufficient food for men and horses for that evening's meal – with fifty goats left over. After one of the most interesting and pleasant days we had spent for a long time and welcome change of diet in the shape of beautiful juicy pomegranates, we had just turned in for the night when the order came to march on Damascus at 4am the next morning. This meant little or no sleep as we would have to be up by 2am to cook some breakfast, feed the horses and break camp.

I was at that time temporarily commanding a Squadron and was delighted to get a message that one Squadron had to remain in charge of the town until the infantry arrived to take over, and that my Squadron had been detailed for the job. When I had handed over to the infantry I was to follow on through Damascus and catch up with the Regiment "somewhere." The bliss of peeping out of my bivouac and seeing the rest of them disappear up the beach was something I had not experienced for a long time. We had another two hours' lie-in and I looked out again and saw the unfortunate sentry still guarding the fifty evil-smelling goats. I was on the point of telling him to get rid of them and get some sleep when I noticed the Red Crescent flying on the fort. It occurred to me that, if we were short of rations, the unfortunate Turks in hospital were bound to be in an even worse plight. So I reverted to my earliest trade – having spent most of my youth driving cattle and sheep for my father's dealing business – and became a drover again.

I drove the goats into the courtyard of the Fort and went inside – where I was met by a spotlessly clean Armenian lady. She took me round the three wards where there were about fifty – equally spotless – night-shirted Turkish wounded, who greeted me with happy grins. I asked her how she was fixed for food and she said "Not a mouthful", and could see no prospect of getting any. She took me aside and said that she actually had about four chapatis – a sort of dry, flat pancake affair – for each man. She had no other help at all and she daren't let them out of her sight for a minute. Every time she left one ward to go to the next, the inmates of the first ward would hop out of bed and turn the place upside down in search of food. I failed to see many hiding-places and asked her where the chapatis were actually hidden. She said "I'll show you" and we went into the ward which appeared to contain the most nimble of her patients.

She clapped her hands and issued some sharp orders, whereupon they all jumped out of bed and out of the ward. She then locked the door and turned up the mattresses, revealing two or three chapatis under each. She told me that this had been her store cupboard for weeks and none of them had been bright enough to look there – or uncomfortable enough to turn their mattresses over. I asked her if she could do with some goats and she was very, very grateful. I called in to see her the following afternoon, just before we started off for Damascus and she assured me that all fifty goats had already been devoured.

En route Acre-Damascus   28.9.1918
(To Paddie at No.17 General Hospital, Alexandria)

"...We had great fun yesterday – The Military Governor of Acre and myself went for a tour around the neighbouring villages just to tell them what good fellows the Englishmen are and how they were to behave etc. We had a sort of pre-runner who used to go on and warn the people and by the time we arrived the whole population would be lined up along the street.

After reading the proclamation the old Sheik would take us off to his home and fill us up with fruit and lemonade. The Persian consul at Acre has a lovely place in one of the villages – a real "fairy garden" – quite the most enchanting and weird affair I ever saw."

3.10.1918

"...we have now travelled some way since I wrote last and are now well on the Damascus road. We spent one night at Nazareth – one at Tiberius and last night under Mount Hermon – had a topping bathe in the sea of Galillee, beautiful fresh water but a very stony bottom (I don't blame anybody for walking on the water). Tiberius is the oldest type of place I have so far seen out here and very interesting – I had the most extraordinary luck – the Military Governors (of both) Nazereth and Tiberius are both pals of mine (one was Clarke that I brought round to the 70th one morning) they both asked me to dinner and produced plenty of Hun wine and champagne which went down rather well after a long and dusty trek."

We left Acre for Damascus as soon as I had handed over. I wanted to get to Damascus during the night as I was afraid of the possible forms of distraction the town might offer. Tom Butler, our Squadron Leader, joined us on the way, so I reverted to a second-in-command and consequently rode at the rear of the Squadron. We reached the outskirts of the biblical town at about midnight and it was lit up like Blackpool. I trotted up to Tom and said "Whatever you do, Tom, don't pull up for any reason whatever. Whether we are on the right road or not let us go through at a fast trot." We started off as I had suggested and I had never seen such a crowd of naughty girls in my life.

Cairo, Port Said or Alexandria had nothing on Damascus in this respect and the girls had, no doubt, said farewell to their German sponsors the day before. Suddenly the Squadron came to a bunched-up halt right in the middle of the town just in front of the "Hotel Victoria" – a sight I least expected to see in such a place. I said to Jack Taylor, "Quick Jack, see what you can find" and gave him a pound note. He was out of the saddle in a flash, run up the steps and was back in a matter of seconds with two bottles of wine, one of brandy and the £1 note.

Tom had not heeded my warning and when he found that he was on the wrong road, had tried to retrace his steps and lead the head of the column back past the rest of us. But the movement failed completely and, before he got back to me, there were more young ladies – in the scantiest of negligee – on the horses than there were Yeomen. In the few cases where some very proper Trooper had succeeded in remaining in the saddle he had at least two of these very cheerful young ladies up with him. The march simply fizzled out and we had to give way to a superiority of numbers. Squadron Sergeant-Major Smart and I found some double doors which led to a sizeable garden, marshalled as many of the Squadron as we could collect, and the garden would hold, and there we bivouacked for the rest of the night. We made our escape at first light and, I am proud to say, "All present and correct." There was no possibility of sleep as Lawrence's villians kept up a furious galloping up and down the "Street called Straight", blazing away thousands of rounds of ammunition the whole night through. Most of the bullets were fired into the air and many fig-tree branches were shot away and fell amongst us. Fortunately, by dawn their jubilations had subsided, and we were spared what I think would have been a dangerous argument as to who had actually captured the town – Lawrence or Lord Allenby.

Left to garrison Acre when the regiment marched for Damascus on 26th September, the progress of "A" Squadron is somewhat difficult to follow as accounts differ and the letters written during the period are not sufficiently specific. The Royal Gloucester Hussars, however, did take part in the triumphal march through

142

Damascus on 2nd October and it appears that "A" Squadron
came through during the next few days. According to the "History
of the RGHY" they rejoined the regiment at Riyaq on 7th October
or 8th. Although Lieutenant Wilson writes to his mother on the
12th October that he is "well and happy", he was already very ill
when the regiment reached Baalbek and was on his way to Beirut
with the other sick when the regiment continued northward to
Homs on the 13th.

Rayak   8.10.1918

"... Damascus is a very decent town but very oriental which
means dirty and dusty, it is surrounded by miles of beautiful
fruit gardens and lovely streams. But the country between
Tiberius and the outskirts of Damascus is far more desolate
than any we have seen. We also came through Capernaum
which is no more than a few ruins and Canaan, where the water
was turned into wine. That was quite a nice place and boasted a
few English speaking Christians who were very hospitable and
pleased to see us.

The winter has not set in yet fortunately but it will soon be
along no doubt. The Xmas pudding was excellent I carried it on
my saddle for nearly 200 miles and we ate it on outpost one
night at Nazareth ..."

Baalbek   12.10.1918

"Just another line to say I'm still quite well and very happy;
this has been a most peaceful war. The Turks either run away
or sit down and wait for us and then surrender.

Letter writing time is very limited as we keep pushing on so
please excuse these very short notes ... We have now got well
clear of the Holy Land, but historical interest is replaced by
fruit, vegetables, fresh meat, wine and every other "conveni-

ence" and the people are far nicer – quite a lot of Christians and no end of them speak good English.

The last week we have spent in the Lebanon Valley – which is very fertile and well-watered, and the scenery and climate take a lot of beating. We are all wondering where we shall spend next Xmas – anyway it will be a better spot than last year. We have got a long way from Alex now and leave will be very difficult I expect ..."

Chapter 10

As Lieutenant Wilson's period of active service came to an end his fellow soldiers in the regiment took the lead in the next stage of the pursuit. They reached Homs on 16th October 1918 to a rapturous welcome from its inhabitants. On 27th October the Royal Gloucester Hussars entered Aleppo – already vacated by the main Turkish force – and eventually took up a position across the road north to Alexandretta to relieve the 15th Brigade who had unsuccessfully engaged the enemy rear-guard. Perhaps fortunately for Allenby, whose men and horses were really in no fit state to go further, Turkey made a separate peace with the Allies on 31st October.

Lieutenant Wilson meanwhile, after some amazing and distressing experiences, had managed to get aboard a hospital ship at Beirut and was taken to the Ras el Tin hospital (apparently a converted Yacht Club) at Alexandria. Whilst there the general armistice of 11th November was declared, and he no longer felt impelled to rejoin the Regiment now policing Aleppo. At Alexandria he was re-united with Paddie who herself spent some time in hospital suffering from Spanish flu.

At the end of the year they were both still in Alexandria, Lieutenant Wilson at Sidi Bish convalescent camp – where he had been sent about 13th November – and impatient for home leave.

I must now relate the saddest period of my war experiences – as it saw the end of my active service and, very nearly, the end of my life. We had chased and chivied the retreating Turk from Damascus to Baalbak with only slight resistance, which was fortunate as we were now suffering very seriously from malaria – a frequently fatal type – which we had, no doubt, contracted in the Jordan Valley. There was no quinine and no medical aid. Several of my friends died and I, myself, was in a very bad way for about two days before reaching Baalbek but I badly wanted to keep going until the Turk threw in the sponge – an event expected at any moment. I just remember sitting on the ground, shivering and shaking and trying to appreciate the wonderful ruins by midnight, covered by two or three blankets that Coombs and Jack Taylor had placed over me. One of them must have gone for the MO, Dr Foster, as he came along and took my temperature and very sympathetically said, "You bloody fool, you've got a temperature of over 105°." Six or seven of us were bundled into an antiquated Ford truck which, in 1918, was about as uncomfortable as anything could be, driven over the appalling roads to Beirut and dumped, on stretchers in an empty school.

There were about twenty of us in that room, and not a soul came to see us until the third night. My Squadron Sergeant Major was lying dead in the doorway and anyone who was fit enough to go for water had to step or crawl over him. A corporal in my troop was dead in the passage just outside. The DADMS* died whilst he was talking to me – in delirium – asking me to remove a jack-knife from his throat, as he had just swallowed it and it was choking him. A subaltern in my Regiment and a good friend of mine spent practically the whole of the time, day and night, shrieking at the top of his voice and jumping up from his stretcher until he finally collapsed.

For the two days and three nights I did not move but the ague caused me to shake to such an extent that my stretcher had travelled half-way across the room. I don't think I ever lost consciousness but I nearly lost hope and I am pretty sure that I should not have seen another dawn if I had not, in the middle of the third night, received a visit from the funniest little man imaginable. I felt someone trying to turn me over and, looking up, saw by the light of the lantern he was carrying, a tiny little negro wearing nothing but a pair of dirty khaki shorts and holding a hypodermic syringe as big as a beer bottle. This he

* Deputy Assistant Director of Medical Services

injected into my behind for what seemed an age but I was too groggy to offer any resistance. Within a matter of minutes I felt entirely relaxed, the shivering ceased immediately and, although my stretcher was no more than a few inches off the floor, I could distinctly hear the sweat dropping on to it – just like a dripping tap. I was naturally very weak and weary all the next day and night, nor could I detect any improvement in the others except from a man called Rance – of the Northamptonshire Yeomanry – whom I had seen somewhere before. We exchanged glances across the room, but that was all we could manage.

No one else came to see us after our "benefactor"; we had no food and it became obvious that we should die if we did nothing for ourselves. I crawled over to Rance and asked him if he could walk. He tried but failed. However he was able to crawl so I said, "Come along then and we will find some food or we shall both peg out." He protested that he had no money but I assured him that I had plenty – which was partly true as I still had my Turkish £25 note. We crawled into the street and sat on the pavement and, to my amazement and relief, along came a tram. I did not threaten the driver but I let him see that I had a revolver in my hand and wanted a ride. He very decently stopped and we climbed aboard – a very odd looking pair of passengers compared to the smartly dressed men and women already inside. Neither of us had shaved or washed for a week and our clothes were in shreds. The driver was most obliging and obviously wanted to help and, by signs, I got him to understand that we wanted to eat. He pulled up in front of a really beautiful hotel and helped us to alight. Rance was a little bashful and seemed to hesitate, but nothing was going to stop me at that stage.

Lunch was being served in an elegant dining room by waiters in tails and white shirts, and the other guests would not have been out of place in a West End restaurant, nearly all wearing

Western dress. We did not make a blustering entry but stood just inside the door and waited for the Head Waiter to show us to a table – which he did most graciously. Soon another waiter arrived with the menu, and another with the wine list. Of course we could not make head or tail of this and we gratefully allowed them to bring us what they thought best. We had a most excellent lunch with two bottles of red wine – our spirits and strength improved with every mouthful – and two huge cigars.

Fortunately most of the other guests had left before the waiter brought our bill. By now I was full of confidence and unfolded my picturesque £25 note. The poor waiter was horrified, he would not even touch it and went to fetch the Head Waiter. He carried on like all the Eastern folk do when they are upset; banged the table with his fists and caused a terrific shindy. We remained unperturbed – full of good food and fairly good wine and with the added satisfaction of knowing that we were not going to die after all.

The note was still on the table when both waiter and head waiter returned with the manager. But now the banging and gesticulating more or less took place among themselves with occasional gestures at the £25 note. We left them to it, withdrew to another room and wrote two or three letters* on their hotel paper. I suppose they did not wish us to enjoy any more of their hospitality for nothing so eventually picked up the note and went away, returning a few moments later with dozens of small grubby notes – also Turkish – as thick as a pack of cards – and handed them to me with a murderous look. This, I supposed, was my change.

By now we could walk with some confidence and, just outside the Hotel, we spotted a barber's shop on the pavement where a jolly old gentleman was plying his trade. He could see that we needed a shave and I told Rance to go first so that I could make a show of generosity by not allowing him to pay, as I would pay for both of us. When we had been attended to I whacked the

* Refers to that written 21.10.1918 to mother (extant)

wad of notes – every one of them – into the barber's hand and he collapsed with mirth, flopping back into one of his chairs. We all had a really good laugh and parted the best of friends, with endless hand-shaking and back-slapping. The shave seemed to do us as much good as the lunch and, in any case, I am firmly convinced that the "worthless" £25 note saved our lives.

We returned to the school feeling happy and thankful, with the intention of rousing anyone else able to move and taking them out to get the same treatment. There was no money of any sort now, but I was not going to let that be any obstacle. However there was no need to put our plan into action for, when we walked into the school, it was completely deserted. There was not a soul in sight and the poor dead had been removed as well. I visited every room without finding a trace of anything – not even a blanket or stretcher. This raised quite a problem. Here we were, two very groggy junior officers without any resources of any kind, in a sizeable town which was, as far as we knew, still full of Turks and Germans*. So we decided to have a rest and see if anything developed. After some time a wicked-looking old Arab crept in obviously on the look out for loot. He was somewhat taken aback when he saw us sitting on the floor and, pointing to the harbour, said, "All gone, big boat."

The harbour was not far away and we could see the hospital ship tied up just at the back of the hotel where we had had lunch. We hurried, as much as we were able, giving the hotel as wide a berth as possible, and arrived just in time to clamber aboard before she set sail. We got a suitable ticking off from everyone in a position to do so, as soon as I reached the top of the gang-way I flopped over the rail to recover from the exertion of the climb. I instantly received a terrific smack in the middle of my back and, turning round, found that it had come from the Matron. She pretended to be very cross and said "I'm not having a tramp like you on my boat, where is the rest of

* Beirut had been occupied by the 7th Division on 8th October so he was actually safe

your shirt?" I then realised, for the first time, that my shirt – my only upper garment – was being held together by only the collar, the rest of it formed a 'V' from neck to waist. This was how I had appeared for lunch at a high-class hotel only a few hours earlier. She told me to stay put until she found me another one and soon returned with a brand new shirt that I kept for many years. I was given a bunk, and was pleasantly surprised when a nurse came round and asked what I should like to drink with dinner. I thought it was a joke but she was quite genuine and I had the choice of red or white wine – or a Guinness.

Actually within half an hour of being on board I was given two demonstrations of how the RAMC acquired the reputation for which their initials stand. As soon as I stepped on the gang-way an RAMC Sergeant Major said, "Your revolver, please Sir". I replied "Not Bernard Shaw likely." I had paid five guineas of my own money for it. Then turning away from me, hands behind his back he said, "In that case you will not be allowed on board." One of the ship's officers could see what was happening and came down the gang-way to explain that no weapon of any kind was allowed aboard a hospital ship, as that could provide sufficient excuse for the Hun to torpedo it. He said a label with my name and Regiment would be attached to it, and that the Sergeant Major would give me a receipt and I should find it at Brigade HQ in a few days. The Sergeant Major very reluctantly gave me a receipt but, needless to say, I never saw my revolver again.

The other incident was very sad and sickening. A young, good-looking boy in the next bunk to mine was in a coma, and obviously only had a short time to live. Under his bunk was a pair of new, very expensive-looking brown shoes. No one came to do anything for him but an orderly stood in the doorway on the other side of the ward, keeping him under observation from a distance. After about an hour the poor boy died and the orderly walked briskly over to the bunk, picked up the shoes and carried them away under a blanket. As far as I can remember, that was all the attention the lad received until he was carried away on a stretcher next morning.

The following letter to Paddie is written on Red Cross notepaper and apparently from hospital in Beirut. There is – understand-ably – some discrepancy between Robert Wilson's recollection in later years and the actual sequence of events.

(to Paddie)   **18.10.1918**

"... you will see that I'm in dock – I have been at the 32nd CCH Beirut for four days – but feel much better today. I have been longing to write to you but I have been a wee bit too groggy with Malaria. I was very fed up when they sent me here but I am glad I came now as I have kept up an average temperature of about 103° or 104° most of the time.

Quite a lot of us have "gone crook" with it – this Hospital is very full but they do all they can for us. They say some of us may be evacuated by boat soon but I think if I could get up and have some fresh air I should soon be fit again."

In his letter to his mother Lieutenant Wilson gives a somewhat different account, obviously to allay any fears she might have as to his well-being. This letter dated 21st October 1918, is one of those which he wrote from the Grand Hotel d'Orient, Beirut on the headed notepaper.

"My dear Mother,

Just a usual report, well and happy, although I have been in dock for three or four days with a touch of Spanish flu but am glad to say I'm quite all right again now and ready to get back to the Regiment. It was really nothing only the Doctor thought it wasn't wise to stay with the Regiment as we were moving on each day with no prospects of making a home anywhere.

I am at the moment feeling "full up of a monsh" owing to a topping lunch at the above hotel and a bottle of local wine to swill it down. Beriut is quite the nicest town we have come across, quite clean and very pretty and the sea and harbour are beautiful – a good tram service and plenty of shops and what's more they will take a Turkish note in payment and as I had a collection of them as souvenirs, I'm all right. I offered a woman in Nazareth a £25 Turkish note for two eggs but she wouldn't take it and I'm glad now as here they take it at ⅛ its value.

We have had no mails from home for some time but no doubt when I get back I shall find some waiting – we have been moving too fast for them to catch up.

The news seems good from everywhere now and the war must come to a finish – you may depend on me not wasting any time in getting home when once it is over, but somehow I don't like leaving the Regiment. I could have got down to Alexandria if I'd liked but didn't really feel bad enough and I should not have been happy.

Must say bye-bye now and go and find out if I can get a boat from here to Tripoli and then get the lorries to carry me to the Regiment who should be some seventy miles east of there – its a blessing we have no luggage on this game or I don't know how we should get about at all."

Ras El Tin Hospital   24.10.1918

"… After writing the letter I returned to the Hospital and the Doctor said, "Look sharp, I want you on board the Hospital ship for Alexandria." Bearing in mind that I must never answer back I picked up my bundle and here I am. We had a lovely trip down

– about thirty hours and lived well – we got here last night. We are in the "Yacht Club" house right on Alexandria harbour a really beautiful place. We only took it over from the Club two days ago.

I am feeling quite fit, but after all, I thought I deserved a rest. I am going to try and find Paddie after lunch, she will be surprised – her Hospital is right the other end of town."

The short sea voyage to Alexandria did us a lot of good and we were sent to the Yacht Club which had been converted into a hospital. Lord Hampton, our Brigade Major, was with us, and soon after our arrival, had a posh gabardine suit sent him by his tailor in London. He tried it on and did not appear to be highly pleased with it. He asked me how it looked and I said "Horrible!" "I am inclined to agree with you" he said "Will you give me a fiver for it?" "No, fifty bob." So I became the smartest officer in the entire hospital, it blended well with Matron's shirt and no one seemed to recognise me as the "hobo" of the hospital ship.

Lord Hampton also had a racing yacht moored at the club, which had happened to be there when war broke out. He woke me early one morning to say that he had arranged a race with some Greek millionaire and wanted me to join the crew. I told him that I knew nothing about this particular sport and, in any case, I was terrified of the sea. He said that didn't matter in the least as I was only required as ballast. He did not give me time to dress and I followed him down to the yacht in my pyjamas. It was all so peaceful and calm and I thought I was going to enjoy myself but, just as we reached the mouth of the harbour – where the Greek was already lolling about in his splendid looking craft – some fool fired a gun, and the race began. Up went canvas after canvas and white horses came aboard. I had been warned that I was only required as ballast and that was exactly how I was regarded by the five or six skilled yachtsmen who comprised the crew. I am sure that, if more buoyancy had been required, I would have been jettisoned and I have never been so frightened in my life. Every few minutes, in response to some order shouted by Lord Hampton, which meant nothing to me, a huge piece of timber would zoom over my head. I suppose I should have responded to this manoeuvering by jumping from one side of the boat to the other, but I was too terrified to move and just hung on for dear life. At one moment my legs would be under water and, at the next, my head. I derived some comfort from the smiles of satisfaction on Lord Hampton's face as the Greek was left further and further behind and convinced myself that if we were about to be wrecked, he would not feel so happy.

All the time we were going straight out to see which was becoming rougher and rougher and the crisis came when we reached the turning point. No one troubled to warn the "ballast" and suddenly we wheeled round on the spot. The piece of timber took its wildest swing at me, as if determined to knock me overboard, and I was completely submerged for some seconds. The journey back was not quite so bad and I recovered somewhat, but not sufficiently to express as much enthusiasm as Lord Hampton. Fortunately by the time the stakes, in the form of vast quantities of champagne, were handed over I was able to bear my full share of the proceedings – but never again!

Ras El Tin Hospital, Alexandria   7.11.1918

"... I am quite fit again but still hanging on and taking life very quietly. We had a yacht race yesterday sailed by officers and naturally we nearly got a wet shirt two or three times, anyway my boat was second which wasn't too bad.

The first batch of released prisoners from Constantinople arrived here yesterday – apparently the Officers had a reasonably good time but I'm afraid the men were treated none too well – we are all anxious to see some of our men return.

So far no mails have reached me, but I should get some now as there have been two or three in the country for some time – but the journey from here to miles beyond Aleppo and back again will make some news a bit stale."

Soon after our arrival at the Yacht Club hospital, the peace of the night was disturbed by someone being carried in on a stretcher, lying on his tummy cursing everyone and everything. He was carried very gently by four men and accompanied by the Matron and a Sister. As he passed my bed I recognised him as the Major in the Worcestershire Yeomanry – a friend of my father, who had done all the sheep and cattle business for his estate for many years. He was lowered inch by inch with the utmost care and finally placed on his bed, still on his tummy, stark naked, and with neither sheet nor blanket to cover him. I went over to him when the "bearer party" had left to ask what the trouble was but there was no need to ask. On his behind was a huge quinine blister which occasionally occured when the injection had not dispersed. The little negro who had cured me at Beirut had apparently given this poor fellow the same huge dose – and nearly killed him. The blister was the size of half a football, he was in a terrible state and, of course, had not received any relief from the malaria. He remained in that position without moving, for a week, and only just survived. When I said that the little negro cured me, I exaggerated a little. What he did was to save my life. I had terrible bouts of malaria for the next three or four years, which coincided with the very hard times the farmers were experiencing in the early 1920's and, during those years, I became very easily worried and depressed.

Sidi Bish Convalescent Home   14.11.1918

"... you will see that I have just left Hospital and come to the above camp. We are very comfortable and happy. I am quite fit again.

Well! The war is over at last, thank God, and it is a relief to know that at least we stand the ordinary civilian's chance of a long life again – there were "some" jollifications in Alex when the news came through – the main streets look like rainbows, practically every nationality is represented and they all stick their respective flags out of every window – most of them however, we pulled down to use in a "General procession" of motors, cabs, perambulators and cab horses, all driven by amateurs."

Sidi Bish Convalescent Camp   24.11.1918

"... I went to the theatre last night with one of our Officers and some civilians he knew in England and enjoyed it very much.

Paddie is much better I am glad to say, but she has had a very rough time this last week, temperature 104° most of the time. I am allowed to go and see her every afternoon and, when she is better, she will no doubt go to a Sisters Convalescent Home for a while.

There is nothing doing in Alex. now, Cairo is more in the swing now winter has arrived. General Allenby arrives there today I think; I hear they are making preparations for a tremendous reception. There is no news of our coming home yet, I hope they haven't forgotten us altogether..."

Sidi Bish Convalescent Camp   17.12.1918

"... Today is a General Holiday and there were to be huge open-air thanksgiving services both here and at Cairo but I'm afraid the weather will put a stop to it.

... Morgan was to have gone home last Monday but was stopped 1½ hours before the boat sailed to make room for a repatriated prisoner and I suppose it is only right.

I have heard no more about my leave but live in hopes of it coming through. GHQ sent and asked me if I would be prepared, in the event of my leave being granted, to be demobilised in England and not return to the EEF – I answered "can a duck swim?"

"We had great "fun" last night – about 3am the heaviest rainstorm I ever knew came along. About 20 percent of the tents went down in the first rush and one side of ours collapsed. I saw it at once but, as it fell on the other fellow's bed, I pretended to be asleep and watched him with one eye open – trying to fix it up. When he had finished and returned like a drowned rat, I rolled over, yawned, and said "Wossup."

Paddie is quite fit again thank you, I am DV meeting her this pm but we shall have to go to some hotel and sit there I expect. I hear rumours that the Regiment are shooting their horses and coming down by boat..."

There is a little matter of interest concerning a small revolver belonging to Paddie which had been given to her by a patient. As far as she knew no one else knew she possessed it. After the Armistice she went on a tour down the Nile to Luxor and was quite mystified to find that, on two or three occasions when the train stopped at a station, she was approached by suspicious looking natives who whispered "Give you five pounds for your revolver Sister." None of the other members of the party was approached in this fashion and the revolver had been in the bottom of her luggage at all times. Some people may remember that the next train to take a sight-seeing party was held up and all the British officers and nurses on board massacred. They surely were the most wicked villains on earth and it is quite a coincidence that both Paddie and I were within an inch of losing our lives to them. In her case, if she had been in the next party and, in mine, if I had not saved one 16-bore cartridge on my pigeon shooting trip early in 1917.

When I was in the convalescent camp near Alexandria in late 1918 we were available for light duty. One day a subaltern came cursing and swearing into the Mess complaining that he had been detailed for Prisoner of War Camp guard for Christmas night. As Paddie was on duty on Christmas Day and I should not be able to be with her, I told him to calm down and I would do guard duty in his place.

At about six o'clock I marched the guard over to the camp and, having relieved the old guard, reported to the Commandant. He turned out to be someone I vaguely knew at home and, although it was not customary for the officer of the guard to dine with the staff, he invited me to join them. I accepted gratefully and there were eight of us altogether, the CO, a Major who was guest for the evening, five other officers of staff and myself.

In the ante-room there were two bottles of sherry which soon disappeared. We then went into the Mess to find a bottle of champagne at each man's place plus four more in the middle of the table. The CO apparently thought it wise to point out procedure while we were still in fit condition to listen. "Now," he said, "You will kindly all drink the bottle in front of you, and then the other four will be passed round. I want every glass to be empty each time the bottle reaches you." These orders were duly carried out. Then two bottles of port arrived, followed by a bottle of Benedictine. I am not sure how much in-road we made into these last three bottles but I have no doubt that most of it was consumed.

The CO was sitting at the head of the table. I was on his right and the guest Major on his left. I was talking quite normally to the CO when, as silently and as easily as a flounder sliding off a fishmonger's slab, he disappeared under the table. The Major, grinning and looking very superior, leant over to have a look at him and did a somersault onto the floor. I had not been paying much attention to the other diners but, when I needed some assistance to deal with the two 'casualties' I discovered that they were not really in any better state themselves. This was about midnight and I had to check the guard posts. I then returned to the Mess but could not get a sign of life from anybody. As a last resort I went into the kitchen to look for some help from the cooks and batmen but this was equally fruitless. Only the CO's servant was fit to help in any way.

My chief worry was the visiting Major. Nobody knew where he came from and I didn't want him to be discovered in this undignified condition. The CO's servant was able to help me get the CO to bed in his own tent. We then returned for the Major, carried him to the same tent, laid him on the ground and poured a bucket of water over his head. Neither he nor the CO had opened an eye during the entire operation.

I kept going to look at them at intervals during the night between visiting the guards and, eventually at 4am the Major was at last able to tell me where he belonged. I organised four men from the guard to carry him the quarter of a mile to his tent.

Sidi Bish Convalescent Camp   26.12.1918

"...We had quite a good Xmas. I went to Church in the morning, then had lunch and called on Paddie in her ward in the afternoon (she was on duty all day), then I came back to camp for Dinner and had a real good one too. The Sisters are having a sort of "Social" tonight so I am going up there after dinner ...I hope you all had a jolly Xmas. I was sorry I did not send you any presents but they ask such ridiculous prices for things, and tell you openly that they put their prices up 25 percent for Xmas .. weather is still top-hole."

Chapter 11

Eventually, on 16th January 1919, Lieutenant Wilson was transferred to Kantara, the assembly point on the Suez Canal used first for the entry, and now for the departure of the Egyptian Expeditionary Force.

Now that the war is over the men are increasingly frustrated and irritated by a delay in their journey home, a frustration apparent in Lieutenant Wilson's letters although he, himself, is at Kantara for only ten days.

From Kantara small boats conveyed the departing soldiers to Port Said for embarkation. Lieutenant Wilson sailed on HMT Caledonian to Taranto in southern Italy. His graphic description of the journey by train through Italy and France, the lack of facilities, poor accommodation and seeming neglect by those in authority now that the fighting man's period of usefulness is at an end, reflect his growing doubts about the future. Interesting too, are his comments concerning attacks on troop trains by the inhabitants of the areas they traverse.

The journey from Cherbourg to Southampton reinforces the "forgotten heroes" theme, further illustrated for Robert Wilson by an incident at Farringdon Market after his long anticipated return home....

After a few weeks in the Yacht Club we were moved to a convalescent camp at Kantara* the spot at which we had first crossed the Suez Canal. This had become a huge base camp through which everything had to pass on the way up to the front line – food, mail, ammunition and reinforcements. A corporal in the Regiment, Ronnie Smith, had been employed at the base for a long time and he recognised me and said he thought he remembered seeing a parcel addressed to me being "chucked"

* The convalescent camp was actually at Sidi Bish (according to the letters he was there from the second week in November until 16th January) and moved to Kantara later on a train going up the line. This was exciting and I asked him to try and retrieve it which he succeeded in doing, and I found a completely undamaged parcel containing a superb Christmas cake sent by a very dear girl friend. There was not a crack in the elaborate icing, it was perfectly fresh and I became very popular. I hate to think what it would have looked like if it had spent three or four days in an open truck, then been thrown onto a camel for another week or more. The odds are that it would never have reached the Regiment. The moment it had been recognised as something to eat it would have been intercepted by our "Berseglieri"* allies who were acting as "lines of communication" troops.

Incidentally you may have wondered how I managed to keep my items of 'loot' until the end of the war, and then get them home. I had collected several shell cases, a saddle, several Turkish swords, the brass saddlery equipment, the Officer's cavalry cloak, a horrid 'saw' bayonet and several other items. These, of course, could not be carried along on my horse so, when anyone from the Regiment was going down the line and having to pass through Kantara, I would ask them to hand anything I had collected over to Corporal Smith. When I was on my way home I found he had everything safely packed away, but I could see no way of getting it home. "Oh, that's easy," he said, and emptied the Regimental Saddler's hamper, a very handsome and stong affair, of its contents. He replaced them with my loot, plastered it with stencilled OHMS lettering and added some undecipherable consignee at Shrivenham station. To my surprise it all arrived safely, and the only cost to me was two shillings and ninepence carriage from Hull to Shrivenham.

No 1 Base Camp
Kantara   **18.1.1919**

"... everyone is getting very restless about this slowness in demobilising and several rowdy demonstrations have taken

* The 'Berseglieri' were actually the crack units of the Italian Army

place. The camp cinema, a huge place, was burnt down two nights ago."

Bill Rickards, that second cousin of mine, who was a corporal in the Regiment, was in the same camp at the time and even more keen on shooting than I was, said he heard that there was some good duck-shooting on the fresh water lakes across the Canal. He could produce a boat, the only things lacking were guns and cartridges! I immediately thought of Ronnie Smith again. He was employed by the Stores where any kit not allowed to go up the line was kept. In no time at all there was a knock at my tent and Ronnie appeared with two rifle buckets – the type we carried on our saddles – containing rifles, and a canvas bucket, as used by mounted troops to water their horses. The rifle buckets contained two beautiful 12-bore guns, taken to pieces and the canvas bucket about 100 cartridges covered by an old forage cap. I was delighted and asked him to send Bill along. He stood outside the tent and, in a very officious voice, shouted out, "Pass it along, Corporal Rickards of the Royal Gloucestershire Hussars, wanted here, at once." When Bill duly arrived there was no difficulty; he stuffed one of the guns down his trousers with half of the cartridges, and I did the same with the rest.

He told me where I should find him with the boat and we had a most enjoyable evening and killed a lot of duck. Ronnie took charge of the lot and said he would arrange for the ducks to be cooked. He knew of an empty hut where we could have a supper party for all the men of the Regiment who were in camp, about fifteen in all. The guns were properly cleaned, oiled and put back in some General's gun cases and, hopefully, he would never know how many cartridges were missing.

Kantara   **24.1.1919**
(To Paddie)

"...I thought I was going today – I heard there was a boat in and they usually send about thirty at a time and I was No 25 and I'm blowed if they didn't send only fifteen. Anyway I am now eighth and should go on the next.

One of our Corporals went duck shooting last night with me, he is a sort of cousin of mine and we had rather better luck, we picked up five and had two more down but they got in the rushes and escaped. We have got a sort of RGH dinner on tonight – quite informal and very irregular as it will chiefly consist of NCOs and men – but it ought to be good fun. We are going to have the duck and someone's pig which 'died'."

To our great joy and surprise we learned the next day that we should be sailing for home in forty-eight hours – officially only on fourteen days' leave but, as the Armistice had now been signed, we felt that we were probably going home for good. Anticipation of the duck supper had until now been sufficient to keep our spirits up but, at the news of our going home, something more substantial in the way of celebration seemed necessary – a few wild duck were quite inadequate. Ronnie was again consulted. "Yes" he had a key to the rum store and he also slept in the canteen to protect the beer! Moreover he had just been given the job of feeding eight suckling pigs the CO had brought the previous day to utilise the swill and waste from the mess tents. Ronnie was only too willing to see the end of them and his new duties. As soon as it got dark the pigs were humanely and silently slaughtered and scalded as porkers. By midnight sixteen Royal Gloucester Hussars – plus the cook-house staff and a few favoured friends – sat down to the most succulent meal any of us had encountered for years. Ronnie Smith had excelled himself in the drinks department and we were still celebrating at dawn when the "other ranks" clicked their heels together and with very serious faces, saluted the few officers in the party, and departed.

Kantara   **26.1.1919**
(To Paddie)

"... And still waiting! and if I don't go in the next week I'll cancel my leave and get local leave to Alexandria. There are rumours every day of boats being in but no orders for us to go. I heard a nutty little yarn last night which I must just tell you – What is better than rising with the lark in the morning? Going to bed with a "WREN"."

28.1.1919

"... I am DV going tomorrow morning on the 'Caledonian' so this will be a good-bye letter."

HMT Caledonian   **29.1.1919**
(To Paddie)

"... I am writing this in Harbour at Port Said in case I get a chance of posting it before I go – we are due to sail at noon today and expect to get to Taranto at 8am on Sunday.

Everyone seems fed up at the prospect of the Railway journey but I don't mind, I think shall rather enjoy seeing the country; of course it will be deuced cold but we have plenty of blankets etc and ought not to feel it much.

Four of us are sort of making up a party for the journey – two of them are on short leave to get married and I never saw two men so absolutely opposite, one is all smiles and as happy as a sand-boy, and the other couldn't be more miserable if he were going to be hanged.

My cousin, Billie Rickards, a Corporal in the RGH is on the same boat and has asked to be my batman. Of course I had to say "Yes." So far his duties only consist of using my bunk when

I'm out, smoking my "baccy" and presenting a small bill when he is thirsty."

We sailed from Port Said for Taranto on the toe of Italy. There were four of us in the cabin and I felt very guilty at the thought of Bill Rickards below decks in crowded quarters. The other three officers agreed that Bill could act as my batman for the trip and appointed someone from their particular regiments to fill the same capacity so that the four batmen could occupy our cabin during the day-time and enjoy the extra amenities.

This was the end of January 1919 and the railway journey from Taranto was as unpleasant as it could possibly be. All the windows in the carriages had been smashed by our "Allies" throwing stones at the previous troop trains. When we stopped at a station there was no food, drink or tobacco available and if you took you eye off a kit-bag for a second it would be stolen. We were in the same compartment for nine days and nights and the cold was intense. I was suffering from a very bad recurrence of malaria and, on the coldest night of all, my travelling companions became very concerned about me. They helped me don every garment I possessed, then, with much shoving and pushing, got me into my "flea-bag." I had a bottle of quinine medicine which I had managed to keep in liquid condition by wearing it under my shirt. It had been removed during my 'dressing-up' and, when one of them noticed it, he told me to keep it in my sleeping bag with me in case I needed it during the night. I woke after a very short sleep and thought I'd better take a dose. It had been in my hand, inside the sleeping bag yet, when I tried to drink it, I discovered it was frozen solid.

We had a small primus stove but very little methylated spirits. It was agreed that this particular night called for the luxury of a fire so the stove was placed on the floor and the other officers formed a ring of feet around it. One – I forget his name – burnt the soles of his boots completely away before enough heat had registered to wake him up. This, indirectly, was a stroke of good fortune for all of us. Shortly after the train pulled into the station at Lyons, we asked the driver how long it would be before we moved on again and he told us "half an hour", so our bootless friend decided to pop into town and buy a pair of boots. He had no sooner left the station when 'toot, toot' and away went the train. This was favourite trick of the drivers and we had to be as active and alert as children playing musical chairs – hardly daring to let go the door handles.

The loss of our friend was somewhat softened by the fact that we had now gained his great-coat, blankets and rations for the rest of the journey. He had backed a winner too – as soon as he realised what had happened he reported to Army HQ in the town and was given money for two nights at a hotel, expenses, a new pair of boots and a first-class ticket to travel by 'Rapide' to Cherbourg. When we arrived three days later, there he was on the platform looking very pleased with himself.

Hotel de L'Etoile, Cherbourg   13.2.1919
(to Paddie)

"... At last we have got here and DV sail for Southampton this evening and should be home tomorrow night. It has been a long and tedious journey and we are all very thankful to say good-bye to the train. You never saw such a mess our carriage was in – all the crumbs and leavings of nine days' meals – we sadly needed a housekeeper.

We found the fellow that we lost at Lyons waiting for us when we arrived this morning, he has had a good tour all over France. I expect the boat will be very crowded but, if there is no room to sleep, we can sit and play bridge all night – I feel as if I shall sleep for hours when I get home. It has been far too cold for pyjamas every night – in fact we have put all our spare kit on top of what we are wearing."

The railway journey had been bad enough but the sea trip to Southampton was even worse. We found that the boat was a horse transport with no accommodation at all, except for the crew. The horse bays had not been cleaned for two or three trips, as far as one could see, and there was about a foot of neat horse dung everywhere. It was bitterly cold with a driving, misty rain and only four people managed to get under cover – myself and three companions of the train journey. We squeezed into the 'Donkey-Steering' room which was already furnished with a lighted lantern in case of emergency and had just attracted my attention.

There was only room to sit down, so the obvious thing was to play cards – which we did – the whole miserable long night. As a concession to a very worried looking 'Tommy' we allowed his parrot to share our room. The poor boy was not at all concerned for his own comfort but was terribly anxious about his parrot and said he was sure it would die if we did not give it shelter. We fixed up a perch for the parrot close to the lantern and he soon put his head under his wing and went to sleep – the only comfortable being aboard.

One of our party, an adjutant in the Black Watch, downed an entire bottle of cognac but his Scots blood was too pure to allow the drink to make him an easier prey, and we failed to extract any money from him.

When we made our farewells at Southampton I asked him what he was going to do after demobilisation. He replied simply: "the same as I have always done: poaching." I was rather surprised that the adjutant of such a famous regiment would consider poaching a suitable occupation and got him to enlarge a little. He solemnly assured me that neither his grandfather, father or himself had ever followed any other calling. Salmon and pheasants were their special line and the most profitable side of the business was supplying hen pheasant for breeding pens to estates throughout the British Isles.

We arrived at Southampton about 5am and hoped to be on our way home in good time; but that was not to be. There was thick fog and the pilots refused to berth the ship until it cleared. So we lay off Southampton for twelve hours – until 5pm – no food, no shelter, not even a cup of tea. This cold, cheerless reception for the returned warriors seemed to set the pattern of the welcome we were due to receive from some of the friends we had left behind when we went off to war.

Farmers had made a mint of money out of the war – there being no excess profits tax at the time – and this had, in many cases, completely changed their way of life and attitudes towards each other. Instead of the warm-hearted hospitality which formerly existed, so many had become greedy and grasping, and vulgarly opulent.

I had only been home two days when I went with my father to Farringdon market. I was still in uniform, not having had time to sort out any 'civvies' and met four former friends of mine all of military age. We were talking in the market when the church clock commenced chiming the tune of a hymn as was its custom at noon. One of them said, "Well, Cheers, see you later on perhaps, but we always go and have two bottles of champagne when the old hymn strikes up." It apparently did not occur to any of them that I, too, might welcome a glass of champagne and I was left standing alone in the market place. I am quite glad that it happened as it always served as a vivid reminder of what money can do to people. I was also uncharitable enough to recall the incident when three or four years later, not one of them had the means to buy a bottle of ginger pop.

I was eventually informed that there was no need for me to rejoin the regiment abroad, as they would soon be coming home and that I would be demobilised in England. I later received a note asking me to call "at my convenience" at some address in Sloane Square, London. I stretched "my convenience" to the limit enjoying the opportunity of travelling to London first class whenever I wished by virtue of that note – which I never handed in. I was on full pay as well and it was not until 28th April, 1919 that I finally decided to be released.

By now I had realised how terribly difficult it was going to be to settle down again. Nothing seemed to have any importance or, perhaps I should say, that my chief grievance was the great importance attached to the most trivial happenings by the folks at home.

My brother Ted returned on 1st May from India in very bad shape. His voyage had lasted for thirty-three days, he had been seasick for thirty-four and was disembarked as a 'stretcher case'. When he became more robust he said to me "Whatever are we going to do? I can't go back to the old routine again." I could see that he was facing the same problems as myself. Anyway for better or for worse I was going to get married and did not know what else I could do to earn a living – other than farming – so I stayed put. Then Ted had a serious illness and, by the time he had recovered, he found he too had slipped into his old groove, and there he stayed.

Thus ended our military careers except for a few years in the Territorial Artillery. It was customary in the Territorials to have alternate 'holiday' and 'shooting' camps. Owing to a general scarcity of shells, guns and horses I only actually attended one 'shooting' camp, enough to leave me with a few memories.

I was acting as GPO (Gun Position Officer) whilst the skipper was at the Observation Post sending his orders down to me which I then transmitted to the gun crews. My only responsibility was to repeat his orders correctly. The Battery was situated in a valley on the Okehampton ranges directly behind a small farm, which an old man was allowed to occupy rent free; on condition that he would 'go to ground' on shooting days and put up with any damage he might suffer. I had been warned that this was the big day, all the big bugs were coming and I was to carry things along as slickly as possible. I received the OC's first string of firing orders ('range', 'angle of sight', 'crest clearance') and repeated them down to "FIRE". At that second I was horrified to see that the guns were pointing straight at the old man's farm. In an emergency everything could be cancelled by "STOP" being yelled through the megaphone. I managed to get this over in time and asked the telephone operator to query range. Range was confirmed and was also correct on the guns. "Query angle of sight" – this was also checked and in order. All that there was left for me to do was query 'crest clearance.'

By now there was a bit of a flap at the Observation Post; the Generals were becoming very impatient, the skipper very angry and the telephone operator shouted, "GPO to the 'phone at the double." I didn't 'at the double' but I went to the phone and he said "What the hell are you playing at, Bob? You have had the order to fire three times and all I get are queries over the phone." I told him that, by looking up the spout of one of the guns, it was obvious that we were either going to blow the old man out of his bed or out of his cellar. Then, very firmly, he said "You have had the order to fire, now go back and fire them, damn you."

I had talked it over with one or two very efficient NCOs who agreed with me but felt that I could not offer much more resistance, especially as the poor skipper, Major TRG Roberts, must have been in a terrible state, surrounded by all that brass. The Major was a wizard with figures and had planned his shoot from the map. His orders could not be totally disobeyed so I compromised by firing one gun only. I was a bit peeved too and, holding the phone so that he could hear, yelled through the megaphone "Right chaps, let her rip." The most extraordinary thing then happened at the farm where, at the back of the house, a sizeable chestnut tree in full foliage was growing in a stone wall. The 18 pounder HE shell hit it at ground level. There was an almighty bang, the tree slowly rose about ten feet into the air and then fell back into the gap in the wall, in exactly the same condition in which it had been growing.

By the time this mishap had been sorted out by those at the Observation Post it was time for lunch and shooting resumed in the afternoon. Things were going quite smoothly when the peace was broken by a shout from the man at the 'phone. "The CO has become a casualty; GPO to the Observation Post at once." This was obviously a conspiracy to get one back on me and I reacted accordingly. The man acting as my horse-holder, George Gill, was actually my groom at home and a very good horseman. As soon as I reached my horse I said to George "I'm going to show them a bit of cavalry stuff. I'm going to dismount at the gallop, on the off-side, so be ready to grab my reins as soon as you see me let go of them." We galloped up the hill and, as soon as I located the Observation Post – with its eight or ten Generals, Roberts and a few signallers, all lying very properly, flat on their tummies in a row – we went hell for leather within inches of the Generals' heels. I dived straight out of the saddle into the midst of them, shouting at the top of my voice "GPO reporting Sir." George Gill played his part well, neither of our horses altered stride for as much as a yard and were out of sight in seconds.

After everyone had recovered from the scare they seemed quite friendly and somewhat amused. The General running the show very quietly remarked, indicating a target about four feet square, "Well, now that you have arrived Wilson, I want you to imagine that that concrete block is a strong machine-gun post and I want it knocked out as quickly as possible."

This was the first time I had been asked to fire a battery and, since my CO was supposed to be dead, I had no idea in which direction the guns had been firing when he had become a casualty. The only thing to do was to tell my replacement GPO to fire one round from No 1 gun. I was peering through my glasses to see the spot where the shell had burst and, after what seemed an age, saw a puff of smoke nearly in the next county and at least three quarters of a mile from the target.

What followed was the most accurate piece of gunnery – and the biggest fluke – ever. I needed a maximum switch in direction and distance, and at best, could only hope to get the next puff of smoke in my glasses simultaneously with the target. I made no special effort at accuracy for the next round, probably about 180 left and plus 850 for range. "No 1 gun, fire." I think the range was 1850 yards. Bang went the gun, buzz went the shell over our heads. I had time to notice the lack of confidence amongst the rest of the party as their glasses were covering a front of a mile or more. The puff of smoke duly appeared in somewhere in my field of vision and, when it cleared away, the top right hand corner of the concrete block was missing. No one congratulated me, but there were gasps of amazement and then the Generals began to laugh with one another. I heard, years later, that it is still called "Wilson's Stone."

Postscript

Robert Wilson and Edith Ross were married in County Down in October 1919 and returned to live and work on Prebendal Farm which he took over upon the death of his father in 1927. There was a short spell in the Territorial Army and four daughters, of whom three survived, were born of the marriage.

These were difficult years for farmers but Robert Wilson survived by hard work and a willingness to experiment and diversify. He developed an important flock of pedigree sheep – some of which were exported to Russia in the 1930s – introduced a dairy herd and mechanised the farm at the earliest opportunity. In 1937 he was able to take on a further 1000 acres and start up two more dairies and was at last prospering when overtaken by the second world war. Added to the burden of running a large farm with fewer hands was the command of a large company of Home Guards, double summer time and wartime shortages. In 1958 he took in his daughter and son-in-law as partners and gradually eased his own work load until finally retiring from the farm in 1969. He died 29th March 1980.

Known as "one of the finest shots in the county" Bob Wilson participated with zest and enthusiasm in all local activities and had a reputation as a story teller. Two collections of his tales of country life, "Just For a Lark" and "The Sparrow Hunters" have been privately printed and widely circulated. A popular and caring man he was supported in all things by his widow "Paddie" who has worked with such faith and tenacity to bring together these reminiscences of his military experiences.